D0643043

CONFESSIONS OF A MIDDLE-AGED RUNAWAY

AN RV TRAVEL ADVENTURE

HEIDI ELIASON

Copyright © 2019 by Heidi Eliason.
All rights reserved.
HeidiEliason.com

Runaway Publishing
Martinez, CA
RunawayPublishing.com

No part of this publication may be reproduced, stored in a retrieval system, or transmitted in any form or by any means, electronic, mechanical, photocopying, recording, scanning, or otherwise, without the prior written permission of the author.

Cover and interior by ebooklaunch.com.

Author photo by Gini Hunt.

Print ISBN: 978-1-7336410-0-5
eBook ISBN: 978-1-7336410-1-2

Library of Congress Control Number: 2019900862

For Cammie, whose strong, independent, and supportive nature made this journey possible,

and

For Mom, who passed on her wanderlust to me, and who understands the dream.

AUTHOR'S NOTE

In writing this book, I relied upon blog posts and notes written during my travels, researched facts when available, and relied upon my own memory and the memories of others. In some places I have condensed events in order to make a five-year journey manageable for the reader.

To protect privacy, the names and identifying information of almost everyone has been changed. Some people I love dearly do not appear in the book at all, but their omission does not affect the substance or veracity of the story. I did so thinking it would maintain peace and harmony, and avoid hurt feelings. Well, you know what they say about best-laid plans going awry.

ACKNOWLEDGMENTS

Writing a memoir can be a scary thing. Many people held my hand and helped bring this book to life. Many thanks to my editor, Aja Pollock. Her professionalism, support, keen eye, and thorough research dressed this book up and made it presentable. Thanks also to Lyn Roberts for her feedback on the first thirty pages.

I am deeply grateful to my dear friend Nancy Hume, who enthusiastically followed my travels, got me started in my first writing group, and whose unwavering support sustained me through difficult times and cheered me through the good ones. Much appreciation goes to my other writing critique partners, Heather Still, Marlene Jackson, Debra Fliehmann, Wiennie McMullen, Melissa Christensen, Matt Vande Voorde, Mark Hagerty, Alicia Watson, and Denise Kalm; and to my beta readers, DeAnn Cossin, Steve Austin, Sherri Wilson Oakley, Rand Stadtman, Barry Hampshire, and Alicia Watson. Without your constructive feedback and support, I might still be fussing with the first chapter.

I owe a debt of gratitude to my sister, Julie, who taught me to love nature and who was my role model in thirsting for adventure. You taught me well, and I still enjoy our adventures together. My parents, Amy, and Gray all helped raise, support, and form the person that I am today, and we shared my first camping and travel adventures. Cammie gave me the encouragement and support I needed to roll off on my own. I love and appreciate you all.

Dan encouraged me, reassured me when I was feeling uncertain, and was the champion in my corner the whole way through. Thank you, Sweetheart.

Chapter 1

The Green Monster

August 2006

Life begins at the edge of your comfort zone.

—Michael Hyatt

I stared at the Green Monster as excitement melted into fear. The driving instructor I'd scheduled for my first behind-the-wheel session had just canceled, and there was no one else to teach me how to drive this gigantic motorhome. Its two-tone green stripes stretched the thirty-foot length of this brand-new, shiny machine. It was something to be reckoned with, and I was about to sign on the dotted line to make it mine. Now all I had to do was drive it over the Rocky Mountains.

I am so screwed.

I paused, took a deep breath, and entered the lobby of the Las Vegas RV park to meet Mike, a friendly guy in his mid-thirties who'd just delivered my motorhome. As we finalized the paperwork for the sale, I peppered the sheaf of papers he presented with my signature, and he handed me the key with a flourish.

"It's all yours now," he said. "Congratulations! Do you have a trip planned, or is it back to work after the weekend?"

"There's no work to go back to. I just quit my job, sold my house, and got rid of all of my stuff. I'm planning to take a year off and travel in the motorhome full-time."

"Wow, all by yourself?" Mike raised his eyebrows.

"Just me and my dog."

"Well that takes guts. Good luck!" He shook my hand and stood up.

As I watched Mike's confident stride toward the door, I remembered the canceled driving lesson. I resisted the sudden urge to throw myself onto the floor behind him and grab his ankles. Except for a couple of brief, white-knuckle test drives, I had never driven a motorhome. The sum of my driving experience involved small Toyotas and Hondas—I had never driven any kind of big vehicle before, and now there was no one available to teach me. This giant was going to tow my car, which meant maneuvering more than forty-five feet of vehicles. To make matters worse, I couldn't back the thing up. Backing up can cause major transmission problems to the towed vehicle when using a tow bar. Being unable to back up the motorhome added twenty more layers of stress to driving something that big. If I pulled into a parking lot or gas station, I had to exit it going forward. Without a driving lesson, there wasn't going to be any training. And now Mike was leaving me alone with the Green Monster.

"Wait!" I called after him.

He turned around, a quizzical look on his face. "Did I forget something?"

"No, I, I—" I stammered as I stalled for time. "I'm just wondering if you have any parting advice for me. You know, on how to handle this thing." I was sure he could hear the hesitation in my voice, smell my sudden fear.

"Don't worry, you'll be fine," he said with a smile. "These things are built really solid. Just have fun."

I exhaled, not realizing I had been holding my breath, and gave him a weak smile. "Thanks." I watched him leave, then went outside to the parking lot, where the Green Monster was waiting for me. I slowly walked the considerable length of the motorhome. "It's just you and me now," I said under my breath. "Behave." The beast was silent.

It was August 2006, and my schedule was tight. I was going to pick up my twenty-one-year-old daughter, Cammie, at the Las Vegas airport the next day and then immediately drive to Minnesota, where I grew up, for a visit with my parents. Cammie only had a week of vacation from her job in the San Francisco Bay Area, so I couldn't wait. With or without instruction, I was on my way, and I had 1,800 miles to drive. I got Rylie, my small border collie mix, from the car and walked back to the motorhome. After settling Rylie into the passenger seat, I walked around to the driver's side.

"You're not going to mess up my plans," I told the Green Monster. I opened the door and hoisted myself into the driver's seat with the help of the grab bar. I peered through the windshield at the cars below me in the parking lot, then glanced over at Rylie, who looked at me expectantly with intelligent brown eyes. His cute face was mostly black, except for a white, freckled patch on the right side of his nose and a thin white streak that ran between his eyes from his nose to the top of his forehead.

"I can see so much better sitting up this high," I said to Rylie. "I think I like this." Rylie looked like he agreed with me. "Hold on, here we go." I took a deep breath, my nostrils flooding with the unmistakable smell of new vehicle and put the key in the ignition. The Green Monster's E-550 engine roared to life. I slid the gear shift into drive and, after repeated mirror checks, eased out of the visitor parking spot. I drove from the parking lot to my campsite without incident and breathed a huge sigh of relief. After three hundred feet, I'd survived my first trip!

I'd wisely reserved a pull-through site, so no backing up was required to exit. I could drive straight through. Even so, with such a wide vehicle, the site felt as narrow as a slaughterhouse chute. I knew that I would be responsible for cajoling the Green Monster over the Rocky Mountains and beyond, to Minnesota. And that was just for starters. My plan was to drive it all over the country. Suddenly, my heart did a triple step.

What have I done? I just sold my house and quit my job! What if I can't get another job? And now I have to manage this monster—I have no idea what I'm doing. What made me think I could do this all by myself?

I thought back to the day my life had tilted and the desperation that had made me take this leap. That Monday had begun like countless other gray, monotonous days, with an hour-long ride on a packed commuter train to my mind-numbing job in San Francisco. As I squeezed as close as I could to the side of the train in my window seat, body odors, coffee breath, and overpowering cologne filled my nostrils. After an hour of willing my mind somewhere else, we arrived at my stop at the Embarcadero Center, and I spilled onto the platform with the rest of the working drones.

While I hurried the three blocks from the noisy underground station to the office, I cast furtive glances at the homeless people I saw chatting, lounging, and leisurely strolling about. This day, especially, I carefully avoided eye contact. I didn't want the homeless to see the overpowering emotion I was feeling, threatening to spill out my eyes and mouth and send my feet running—anywhere; it didn't matter as long as it was away from where I was headed. Envy. I felt pure envy. I envied the homeless people.

Somewhere, in the more rational part of my mind, I knew this was crazy thinking. Homeless people were not to be envied; they should be thought of with compassion, or maybe pitied. They were drifters, living in dangerous and cruel conditions, with countless challenges and problems, some of which might be insurmountable. Yet all I could see that day was their seemingly endless freedom.

The homeless had no daily eight to do in a cramped cubicle, repeating the same routine day after day for just enough money to pay the mortgage and bills. They didn't spend two or more hours commuting every day for this daily dread and had no homes and yards to repeatedly clean and tend on the weekend as the clock ticked louder and faster toward Monday. Time was a limitless commodity for them; there was no rushing around and squeezing too many activities into too little time. At least, this is the way it seemed in my tilted world.

If I were homeless, I fantasized, I would have a community of like-minded people to spend unhurried time with, and no schedules, deadlines, or limits. I could go wherever I pleased and do whatever I felt like doing that day—and every other day. I could catch my breath and relax. I would be rich with the only currency that mattered to me: time. The lifestyle seemed so unencumbered, so . . . enticing. I wanted to escape from the hamster wheel. My life was a marathon that never ended, and I was worn out. I wanted freedom.

Somewhere along the way I'd bought into the notion of the American dream—the traditional model of success. Find a job that pays well, get married, buy a house and all the trappings. Do my part to be a cog in the wheel that keeps our capitalist society going. Be satisfied with a measly few weeks of vacation every year—the time when I really came alive and felt happy. It took me decades to realize that the life I'd chosen for myself made me miserable.

Added to my misery was my realization that I was born with wanderlust. Routine is not my friend, and I need new experiences to satisfy my curiosity, restlessness, and thirst for adventure. Too much of things staying the same makes me feel like a caged animal, pacing back and forth, the need for movement all-consuming. I longed for travel. When I traveled, I woke from my routine-induced slumber and came alive. Aside from Cammie, it was the spark that fueled me. But still, envying the homeless? Clearly, I was unhinged. I desperately needed a change—a major life transformation. I needed to reclaim that lost part of myself that came alive when I traveled.

When the realization hit me that I could sell my house for double what I'd paid for it and have the time and freedom to do whatever I wanted, at least for a little while, it was as though a huge door was thrown wide open. Sunshine came rushing into the dank, dark corners of my depressed mind. Above the door was a large, brightly lit sign that read, "Exit."

It had taken nearly a year to get ready, but my hope and anticipation grew with each stage of my preparations. Now I was finally walking through that exit. I'd been so excited to embark on this journey, it hadn't occurred to me that I might feel terrified when the dream became a reality and I was finally hitting the road. But here I was, officially the owner of the Green Monster, and my legs felt rubbery. My new life was starting, ready or not.

My first task was to feed the beast. Before I could do that, I needed to unpack one of the boxes that littered the floor of the motorhome. A couple of weeks earlier I'd sent several boxes of dishes, pans, and other household items to the motorhome manufacturer to put in the motorhome and be delivered to me when the sale was finalized. I emptied one of them so there was enough room on the floor to walk.

After I unloaded some kitchen items and arranged them in the small cupboards, I squeezed past the remaining boxes and made my way to the driver's seat. I started the engine and slowly rolled out of my campsite and onto the road of the RV park, looking twice in each direction. From there I turned onto a four-lane road to find a gas station, tightly gripping the steering wheel. I felt sorry for anyone who was following behind me that day. I didn't dare take my eyes off the road long enough to look at the speedometer, but I was probably driving ten miles per hour.

I maneuvered the motorhome next to a gas pump without my tail crashing into anything, unclenching my jaw and peeling my fingers from their claw-like grip on the steering wheel. The motorhome felt very long, and it had quite a tail swing when turning. I inserted my credit card into the pump and started the gas flowing into the tank. After what seemed like an eternity, the pump stopped and my eyes nearly popped at the $75 price tag. I'd always owned economical cars and had never come anywhere close to putting $75 worth of gas into a tank before. *Welcome to the RV lifestyle.*

Even more distressing, when I started the engine, I discovered I didn't even have a full tank of gas. The pump apparently had a $75 maximum for credit card purchases, but being new to the world of big-bucks gas pumping, I didn't know this was how it worked. I figured I had to go to another gas station to fill the tank. Dumb blunder number one.

I lumbered down the road at the terrifying speed of about twenty miles per hour to the next gas station, my newly stowed dishes and pans rattling and crashing about in the cupboards. I made a mental note to secure them inside the cupboards when I got back to the RV park. At the next gas station, I filled up the remainder of the tank. One of my RV friends later told me that all I had to do was put the credit card in again when I reached the maximum—there was no need to go to another gas station. What's the point of a dollar limit if you can just put the card in again? Obviously, I didn't understand high-price gas-pump protocol.

After carefully making my way back to the RV campground and getting the Green Monster safely parked and reconnected to the various hoses and cords, I flopped onto the sofa, worn out from the stress of handling such a large vehicle. *How am I going to drive this thing halfway across the country in just a few days?* My stomach cartwheeled as I thought of what it might be like dragging a house on wheels with a car tail over the Rockies.

Fear wasn't part of my plan. I'd thought I was prepared, and I'd done my homework. I'd learned about tires, converters, inverters, batteries, propane tanks, generators, sewage tanks, water tanks, water pumps, tow bars, base plates, and leveling blocks. Then I'd learned about electrical hookups, solar panels, the supplemental braking system, the CB radio—and that was just the beginning of the extra-gadgets wormhole. There were tire stem extenders, tire pressure monitors, sewage tank monitors, electric levelers, air compressors, battery fillers—the list went on and on. The sheer volume of things I learned—and still needed to learn—was overwhelming. I had begun to wonder if I would ever be ready for "full-timing," as living and traveling in an RV was called.

Fortunately for me, there was a school for RVers, called Life on Wheels. Four months earlier, I'd attended three days of classes on a college campus in Tucson. I'd learned about everything from dumping sewage tanks to simple RV repairs. On the third day, I walked into a class for solo travelers and sat down at a desk near the front. Across from me sat a stocky woman with short, honey-brown curls, a dash of freckles, and a friendly smile. She looked to be around my age, forty-five, which was unusual. Most of the RVers I saw were of retirement age and beyond. She must have read my mind, because when the class was over, she leaned toward me.

"We don't really fit in with this crowd," she said in a low voice, her head nodding toward the rest of the people in the room. "I think we're the youngest ones here—by a decade or two." She gave a hearty, infectious laugh, and I liked her immediately.

"I would say they have a healthy head start," I agreed, grinning. "I can't wait that long." Retirement age was much too distant a target for me. I needed to go *soon*.

"Me neither. I just got my motorhome recently, and I'll be hitting the road in a couple of months."

"I should be ready in about four months, if my house sells."

"What kind of RV do you have?" Cindy asked.

"I don't actually have one yet. I'm thinking about getting a motorhome but haven't decided. I thought coming here might help me make up my mind."

"Good idea. I'm Cindy, by the way."

"Heidi. Nice to meet someone my age."

"What made you decide to hit the road?" Cindy asked.

My mind quickly traveled over the past three decades, and the years of financial hardship, working two jobs, raising Cammie on my own, and the loneliness. I remembered how I'd envied the homeless.

Instead I said, "I needed to get out of the rat race, and I've always wanted to travel. A year-long road trip seems like total freedom." That was true, but if I were being totally honest, I would have told Cindy that I was running away to save my life. I was taking a break from the conventional "American dream" for a solo journey to recover my spirit. "What about you, what made you decide to hit the road now?"

Shoulders back, Cindy looked me straight in the eye and didn't blink. "I got a brain tumor." When she saw the stricken look on my face she said, "It's okay, it was benign, and they removed it. But it made the decision to hit the road easy. I've always wanted to do this. I decided I wasn't going to wait until I retired, so I sold my condo and quit my job."

We talked for a while and exchanged contact information, agreeing to keep in touch and meet up somewhere on the road. Cindy was the first of many gutsy women I met and admired during the course of my travels, all of whom made a big impression on me.

If Cindy can do this, I can, too.

After all of the months of research and the education I received from Life on Wheels, internet forums, and other people I talked with, I went from empty bobblehead blonde to RV Einstein, spouting the theory of tire pressure relativity. I figured out what kind of motorhome to buy, which towing package to get, what other equipment I might need, and which clubs to join. But as I soon found out, there was still so much I didn't know.

After returning from feeding the beast, I continued unpacking the boxes that contained the little that was left of my possessions, and stowed things away in all of those tiny cupboards, drawers, and bins. Getting rid of my furniture and most of my clothes, books, dishes, and knickknacks when I sold my house had made me feel lighter, freer. I hadn't realized how much all of my stuff weighed me down. The only things I had to force myself to part with were my books. I collected books and had more than seven hundred when I sold my house. I would rather get rid of clothes than books. I kept some of the special ones signed by the authors, but there were still so many, and each one pulled at my heart as I sold them or gave them away. I carefully placed one of my remaining boxes of books in an outside storage compartment of the motorhome and put the other in the trunk of my car, feeling comforted by the fact that they were still with me.

That evening I was so busy preparing for my trip and getting settled, I didn't have time to visit with the neighbors or fully process the first night of my new lifestyle. It was late when I dropped into bed, exhausted, and immediately fell asleep. Fortunately, thoughts of what could go wrong the next day were far from my mind.

Chapter 2

Hitting the Road

August-September 2006

Before anything else, preparation is the key to success.

—Alexander Graham Bell

After a stress-free drive in the car to the airport the next morning, I picked up Cammie. Only a few days had passed since I'd left her in the Bay Area, but I was excited to see her. As soon as I saw her long blond hair, warm brown eyes, and bright smile, my fears were forgotten.

"I'm so happy to see you, and so excited that you're coming with me for my first trip in the motorhome," I said, giving her a big hug.

"Me too! I can't wait to see it."

We planned to hit the road right away, so we returned to the RV park to install the tow bar, hook up the car, and drive to Minnesota. After Cammie and Rylie had a happy reunion, I gave her a quick tour of the motorhome.

"Look how clever they are at using the limited space," I said. I showed her the bedroom and the storage drawers beneath the queen-sized bed, with a small closet on either side. The shower was separate from the tiny room containing the toilet and sink, and the door to the shower could be opened fully and latched, closing off the bedroom from the rest of the motorhome.

"It even has a pantry." I opened the handle on the nearly full-length mirror on the other side of the shower door to reveal four shelves for canned goods. There was a three-burner propane stove with an oven, and a little shelf that folded up for counter space next to the sink.

"Not much counter space," Cammie observed.

"No," I agreed. "But I'm not crazy about cooking anyway. This is where you'll sleep." I showed her how the sofa converted to a double bed. "You can watch TV in bed." Across from the sofa was the dining table.

"The dining table folds down the side of this small cupboard for more space in the living room, or we can lift the tabletop to seat two. Look, there's even a wine rack down below. If you open the inside of this cupboard, there's a table leaf stored inside. The table will seat up to five people with the leaf added."

"Pretty cool, and it feels a lot roomier in here when it's all folded up," Cammie said.

"What I love best are all of the windows," I said. "They're big and they're on all four sides of the motorhome, which makes me feel like I'm outside."

"It's really nice, Mom. This will be fun!" With the tour over, we went outside to install the tow bar so we could start our trip.

The base plate for the tow bar and supplemental braking system had already been installed on the car a couple of weeks ago, but installing the tow bar on the motorhome was up to us. I wasn't concerned. I had been told it was easy.

We got the tow bar installed on the motorhome, thanks to the step-by-step instructions. Eager to help, Cammie knelt down to attach the safety cables from the base plate on the front of the car to the underside of the motorhome.

"Ah, Mom? We have a problem. The cables aren't long enough to reach the motorhome."

"What? How can that be? Did we do everything right?" I got on my knees to peer at the cables under the motorhome. They were about four inches away from the attachment point.

We read the instructions again and checked our work. We'd followed them perfectly. I felt my blood pressure rise and my skin prickle with perspiration. No one had mentioned the possibility that the safety cables might not be long enough. All of that time spent at Life on Wheels felt like a complete waste. *How can I live my dream if I can't get the car hooked up to the motorhome? Now what do I do?* The Green Monster was thumbing its nose at me, misbehaving already. I instantly went from RV Einstein back to bobblehead blonde.

Then I remembered there was a Camping World in Henderson, about a half-hour drive from where we were staying in Las Vegas. Camping World not only sold camping gear and RV supplies, they also offered service. I called them to see if they could offer any suggestions for getting me out of this pickle and fidgeted while I explained my problem to a guy in the service department.

"What you need are cable extensions," he said. "We get these calls all the time. I don't know why those cables aren't longer. We have them in stock if you want to come and get them."

I felt my muscles relax and sighed with relief. Problem solved. Cammie and I drove to Henderson in the car, bought the extensions, and headed back to Vegas. By the time we installed the extensions and hooked up the car behind the motorhome, it was two p.m. Now I was faced with getting onto the freeway with this ginormous rig. *Here we go.*

After easing onto the busy freeway, I kept glancing nervously at my side mirrors as the cars and trucks barreled up next to me. The first time a big rig passed at top speed, the wind slapped the motorhome like a hockey stick smacking a puck.

"Whoa," Cammie exclaimed as I fought to keep the motorhome in my lane. "That wind is strong!"

I clenched my teeth, gripped the wheel, and clung for dear life, adrenaline jumping through my veins. *Is this what it's going to feel like every time a semi passes?* After about two hundred miles, my shoulders ached from clutching the steering wheel so tightly. I decided to stop for the night.

As soon as I found a campground and got parked, Rylie came out from the floor of the passenger seat, where he'd slept while we were driving, tail wagging. This turned out to be his routine every time I drove the motorhome. Driving time was nap time, but he was always eager to go outside and explore once we got parked. He loved all of the new smells and opportunities for marking territory.

As Cammie and I walked Rylie I said, "I've decided we're only staying in campgrounds with pull-through campsites on this trip. There's no way I'm going to worry about unhooking the car and backing into a parking spot after running the freeway gauntlet every day." This turned out to be a smart decision. Every day we got to our campground after dark, and one night, not until ten thirty p.m.

There was no leisurely sightseeing on this trip, because we needed to get Cammie to Minnesota to see my parents before her vacation was over. That meant driving 1,800 miles in a few days. I gazed longingly at the signs for the national parks that I wanted to see as we blazed past. I comforted myself with the knowledge that I would come back soon.

Each day, in spite of our good intentions, we got a late start. It seemed to take a long time to prepare for blastoff. I was still getting used to operating this complicated contraption. I was learning not only how to drive the monster, but also how to connect and disconnect all of the hoses and cords, fill and dump tanks, check monitors, and measure the pressure of all six motorhome tires and fill them with air, plus everything else that needed to be done. I was learning that motorhomes always have something that needs to be filled, emptied, monitored, or maintained. Still, I was gaining confidence as I became more comfortable with the daily tasks.

As we entered the state of Colorado, I started to feel a bit more comfortable behind the wheel. Then we hit the Rocky Mountains. Climbing to Vail Pass at nearly eleven thousand feet was like being a snail racing in the Indy 500.

"Can't this thing go any faster?" Cammie asked as cars kept whizzing past.

"I have the gas pedal all the way to the floor. I can't seem to get more than forty miles per hour." I barely noticed the beauty of the rugged, snowcapped Rockies as I anxiously watched vehicles zooming up behind me. I got to know my flashers quite well and hawkishly watched the temperature gauge to make sure the engine wasn't overheating. But as I soon found out, going up the mountain was the easy part.

What goes up must come down, and descending a steep and winding mountain road with seventeen thousand pounds of motorhome was like a scary roller coaster.

"I hope I'm not riding the brakes too much," I told Cammie. "I have it in low gear." I hunched forward, my foot tense on the brake.

"Well, at least they have runaway truck ramps here," she replied, trying to reassure me.

I was not reassured. When I finally saw the Rocky Mountains in my rearview mirror, I breathed a huge sigh of relief. "We made it over the Rockies!"

Crossing Nebraska was monotonous, with endless, parched-looking fields filling the miles. We headed north to South Dakota and then east to Minnesota. Once we got on I-35 and started heading north again, I was in familiar territory. The green cornfields and golden-brown prairies of the southern part of the state eventually gave way to the lush woods and cobalt-blue lakes of the north. This stark difference in scenery always made the state seem like two different countries. My excitement grew as we neared Duluth and my childhood home. We were both eager to see my parents.

My dad, a former auto mechanic and race-car driver now in his seventies, still considered himself the expert on anything with wheels. After big hugs with him and my mom, a soft-spoken woman a few years younger than my dad, he directed me as I got the motorhome parked in their driveway. I gave him and my mom a quick tour of the inside.

"You have everything you need in here and it's so nice," my mom said, worry clouding her big brown eyes. "But it's so huge. Can't you just travel around in your car?"

"No, Mom. I'm going to be living in it. I can't live in my car." I could tell by my dad's frown that he had some reservations, too. "What's the matter, Dad?"

"I used to work on these things years ago," he said, concern etched on his face. "They break down all the time."

"That was a long time ago," I said. "They're made better now. Don't worry, I'll be fine." I could see he wasn't convinced.

For the next few days, Cammie and I had some much-needed rest and relaxation, nestled in the woods with my parents. Each time I visited the place where I grew up, I was comforted by the lush, green foliage that enveloped me. Those few days with Cammie and my parents felt more precious with each passing hour. I was feeling especially anxious about leaving Cammie.

"I'm really going to miss you," I told her. "I feel like a bad mom, taking off on this adventure without you. I feel like I'm abandoning you."

"You're not being a bad mom, and you're not abandoning me," she said. "It's about time you got out of the rat race and had some fun. This is the perfect thing for you. You've worked really hard for it. I'll miss you too, but we'll get to see each other often."

I gave her a hug, relieved, and grateful for her support. She was right; I had worked really hard for this. For most of my life since I was eighteen, I'd either worked two jobs, worked full-time and gone to college part-time, worked overtime, or had a business on the side. I'd worked that hard in order to make ends meet.

From the time Cammie was born when I was twenty-four, I'd raised her on my own. There were no breaks for visitations with her father, because she didn't meet him until she was in college. We married when I was twenty-one, after a brief courtship of hurried pursuit. I allowed myself to be caught up in Steve's enthusiasm and the flattery of his persistent attention. He proposed four months after we met. It seemed romantic and exciting to my young, naïve mind. I didn't realize then that I was just one of a string of brief impulses he would have throughout his life.

Two years into our marriage, Steve started having angry outbursts over minor frustrations. He got mad at me and was worse with the dogs. Then he started throwing things. One day we were working in the backyard of the new home we'd bought, installing fence boards. Steve was having a hard time hammering the nails into the boards, getting angrier each time a nail bent.

"You're not holding the boards the right way."

"Well, how do you want them? This is how you told me to hold them."

He tried hammering another nail, and when the nail bent, he threw the hammer across the yard.

"I'm taking a break," I said, feeling like one of the nails, and marched into the house. I didn't want to be around him when he was like that.

Another time he was in the hallway of the upper level of our open, split-level home, trying to fix the vacuum cleaner. Once again, he got frustrated and angry, and threw the screwdriver across the living room, where I was sitting. The screwdriver hit the front door, narrowly missing the glass pane, and the dog sleeping below.

"Steve!" I yelled. "You almost hit Molly and just missed the window." An argument followed.

"I don't know if I love you anymore," he said.

"You're becoming a stranger," I responded as he slammed the door on his way out. This wasn't totally true. He had always been a stranger—I wasn't with him long enough before we got married to really know him. I realized then how hard I was trying to fit into this new life with Steve. I felt scared and confused. *This isn't the man I thought I married. Do I want to spend my life with him?*

When Steve returned I said, "I think we need some counseling."

"We can't afford it," he said. End of discussion.

I trudged up the stairs to the bedroom, defeated, then cried myself to sleep.

I discovered I was pregnant at about the same time. I felt a confused tumble of emotions. We had been trying to start a family for months, but I was having a hard time getting pregnant—until suddenly I wasn't. Knowledge of the pregnancy did nothing to repair the situation with Steve. Before our relationship started to crumble, I had been so excited to have a baby, but I knew I couldn't raise my child with this angry man. After giving it a lot of thought and talking to my parents, I made a tough decision. One night after work, I dug up my courage.

"I'm leaving," I told Steve. "I'm moving back to Minnesota."

"I don't think you should go."

"Why not?" I asked. I held my breath, waiting for his response. I wanted him to tell me that he still loved me and wanted to work things out.

"I just don't."

I exhaled, the hurt and disappointment deflating my entire body. "Well, I need more of a reason to stay than that. I don't want to live with someone who is impulsive and angry."

After first meeting with a divorce attorney, I packed up whatever I could stuff into the back of my small Toyota, put my dog in the front seat, and left our home between the rugged mountains and wheat-colored plains of Colorado. I loved Colorado and had been so excited to move there when I was twenty, but I needed my family now. I headed back to the quiet beauty of Duluth and moved in with my parents, who welcomed me with open arms.

From the moment she was born, the compass of my life always pointed to Cammie as my true north. I loved her with all my heart and worked hard to give her a good home and experiences that would enrich her life. Maybe subconsciously I was trying to make up for the absence of a father in her life. I wanted her childhood to be as normal as possible, and to allow her the same opportunities kids from two-parent families had. The divorce was final when Cammie was six months old, and although Steve kept saying he would come see her, he never did.

When Cammie was almost two years old, I visited California's San Francisco Bay Area. There, I fell in love—with the state. I felt like I belonged in California. This was a place of great beauty and endless possibilities. The sun skittered over the ocean under a boundless blue sky, while bridges laced the cities across the bay to San Francisco, beckoning me to come and play. Snowcapped mountains were only a few hours from the beaches, with sweet-smelling orange trees and succulent strawberry fields in between. Opportunities were as plentiful in California as the red, white, and pink oleander that lined the streets and highways. Whether it was work, education, culture, or recreation, the choices were endless. I felt the seeds of hope starting to bud inside me. It was very different from the cramped opportunities in Duluth that nudged people to long nights on bar stools next to cigarette-littered ashtrays.

"Someday, we're moving to California," I told Cammie.

When Cammie was three, I arranged job interviews in California, and we combined a fun-filled Disneyland trip with more serious job hunting. I received a couple of offers, one in San Francisco and one in Walnut Creek, a small city about twenty-five miles east of San Francisco. I thought the suburbs would be a better place to raise a child, so I told Cammie, "We're moving to Walnut Creek!" We arrived three weeks later. But there was a price to pay for living with beauty and possibilities.

I was thrilled when the salary for my legal secretary job paid double the salary I'd made in Duluth. Unfortunately, I soon realized that living expenses were triple what I was used to paying. Even McDonald's was more expensive. I worked harder.

Sometimes I didn't get child support from Steve for years at a time. When I did get it, the amount was so meager, it didn't pay for much. The worst period was the two years when I worked driving a paper route in addition to my full-time job. I woke up at three a.m., loaded Cammie into the backseat so she could sleep, and drove around for two hours delivering newspapers. I slept for a half hour after we got back home before I woke again to get Cammie to school and me to my main job. The paper route was seven days a week, three hundred sixty-five days a year, but at least on the weekends I didn't have to work my office job.

At the end of the two years I was exhausted and depressed. All I wanted to do in my free time was sleep. I hated working two jobs, but we needed the money. Over the years I worked at jobs that deadened my senses and made me feel trapped, in order to support my little family and, later, my mortgage. I was running the hamster wheel and could only focus on the next couple of steps. I couldn't see that there was a big, beautiful world beyond the cage.

After Cammie graduated from high school, she decided to go to college in Fort Collins, Colorado. It was a friendly little city with a pretty college campus full of old brick architecture and the beautiful Rocky Mountains nearby. She would be safe there. I was excited for her to experience college life but couldn't help but feel my heartstrings pulled tight as we got her settled into her dorm room. I bought her a bike and choked back the tears as we unpacked her clothes and put them in her closet and drawers. *Don't fall apart.* I tried to comfort myself with the thought that she would be home for Christmas in a few months.

After Cammie was gone about six months a heavy weight, like an enormous boulder, rolled over and flattened me. The realization hit me that I was alone. My true north was an adult, and she had her own life without me. I was an empty-nester, and when I looked in the mirror, what I saw terrified me. The face staring back at me belonged to a middle-aged woman with lifeless eyes who didn't know what she wanted to do with the rest of her life.

"Who are you?" I asked the strange face in the mirror. I saw an endless procession of days, weeks, and months with nothing much to look forward to except loneliness, loss of purpose, bone-wringing fatigue, and a romance-starved existence. The water-torture job, hours of commuting, endless yard work, and home maintenance drained the spirit from me with very little fun to refill my energy coffers. My life had centered around Cammie for so long, I didn't know how to handle living without her and be on my own. It had been more than twenty years since I'd lived without her constant companionship, and I was overwhelmed by the deafening quiet and emptiness. I should have been excited about this new phase, but instead, I felt lost in the woods without my compass.

In 2004, I received a phone call from Cammie in Colorado. "Mom, I want to stay in Colorado for Christmas. I've been invited to spend the holiday with Mark's family. Is that okay?"

Mark was the new boyfriend Cammie had met in Fort Collins. My shoulders slumped as I struggled with my response. I remembered how as a little girl, Cammie always held tightly to my hand wherever we went. Even when she was past the age when I worried she might run off into danger, she automatically latched on to my hand. Later, when she was in high school, she would come into my bedroom as I sat in bed reading before going to sleep. As she stretched out on her stomach next to me, we would talk about everything and nothing.

Now my little girl was pulling her hand away, and I felt the cold vacuum of empty air. I had known that this emotional separation would come, that it was necessary even, but knowing that didn't make it any easier. I knew the days of bedtime girl talk were gone.

"Okay, honey. I'll miss you, of course." Somehow, I managed to make it through the rest of the conversation before the tears started their well-run trails down my cheeks. I didn't want her to know how much I had been counting on her Christmas visit to lift my spirits, and how much I wanted my compass back.

A heavy gray cape descended over me, and I couldn't shake it loose. I had always been a sensitive person, and things hit me hard. In the fog of my loneliness and depression, I couldn't think of anything to look forward to in life. *What is my purpose now? What does life hold for me other than hard work and loneliness?*

Although my friends and family knew I was depressed during this time, I didn't tell them how bad it really was. I was ashamed that I couldn't be grateful for my life. It was the life I had chosen, more or less, and there were no terrible tragedies. But sometimes the dripping erosion of joy can be more damaging than a sudden, traumatic event. I couldn't seem to escape from the flattening depression. I began suffering from burnout and an emotional paralysis that left me desperate for something positive to pull me up and out of my self-imposed funk. I saw nothing in my future that would muster up some passion, meaning, or fun in my life. I started having strange health issues that the doctors struggled unsuccessfully to diagnose. First some unexplained bumps appeared on my hands and then my bladder was bleeding. I suspected they might be stress-related conditions, and that suspicion was seemingly confirmed when they later disappeared just as mysteriously as they had come. I sought counseling from a therapist during this time and although it helped to talk to someone about my feelings, there were no major breakthroughs in my depression.

I began to fantasize about leaving everything behind and running away to the beach somewhere with an Airstream trailer. That's when I started envying the homeless. Even when Cammie moved back to California with her Colorado boyfriend in tow, the escape fantasy continued. I wanted a different kind of life than the typical "American dream" could offer.

Now here I was, escaping the hamster wheel for a life of freedom. Except instead of an Airstream trailer, I had a motorhome. But I was still struggling with leaving Cammie behind. I drove her to the Duluth airport to return to her job and school in California and gave her a big hug. "I'll be seeing you at Christmas," I promised. "That's only a few months away. But you can call me anytime, and if you need me, just say the word and I'll come back."

"Don't worry, Mom. I'll be fine. Have fun!" Even though she seemed confident, I still felt a twinge as I watched her board the plane. On the drive back to my parents' house, I tried to distract myself from the sadness by focusing on my next trip.

In a couple of weeks, I was driving to New Mexico to meet up with Cindy, the woman I met at Life on Wheels, and some of her RVing friends at the Albuquerque balloon fiesta. But I didn't realize what scrutiny I would be under when I arrived.

CHAPTER 3

FITTING IN

OCTOBER 2006

It's easy to fit in. And it's also the easiest way to lose the precious parts of you.

—Anne Bechard

"You'll call me when you get to the campground tonight, right?" my mom asked as she hugged me goodbye. "To let me know you made it okay?"

"Yes, Mom, I'll call you," I agreed. Little did I know that this would become a regular request whenever I drove to a new camping spot. Driving always made my mom nervous, and I'm sure the hulking Green Monster and my lack of experience did nothing to calm her fears.

I had already backed the motorhome out of the driveway and hooked up the car, so I could pull straight out onto the road. As I headed toward Interstate 35, I felt an unusual mix of apprehension and anticipation. I was really on my own now. No more navigation help from Cammie when the GPS led me astray. I already missed her help filling tires and doing the many tasks that had to be completed every time I prepared to hit the road or settle into a campsite. Most of all, I missed her cheerful companionship. Rylie was snoring softly under the passenger seat, and in spite of the Green Monster's customary low roar, it seemed very quiet. I slipped a CD into the player and sang along. As the miles rolled under ten tires, my excitement grew. *I'm officially beginning my solo journey!*

Albuquerque was 1,400 miles from Duluth, so there were three days of driving ahead of me. I followed I-35 south through the thick cornfields and hay-filled farms of southern Minnesota and Iowa, with only an occasional barn or herd of cows to break the monotony. More green and gold scenery whizzed past as I cut across the corner of Missouri and into Kansas, focused on my destination. I stuck close to the freeway and made quick overnight stops at RV parks nearby, getting pull-through campsites to avoid unhooking the car. This allowed for a faster departure in the morning. I was still getting used to managing the Green Monster. Slowly but surely, I was getting faster and more efficient, and my confidence was growing. Everything went smoothly until I hit Oklahoma.

This was my first encounter with toll roads. Paying to drive on a highway was new to me. I was familiar with paying to cross bridges in the Bay Area, but not to drive on freeways. As I was leaving the RV park, the GPS failed me. As I dutifully followed the spoken commands through the maze of streets and freeway entrances, I realized too late that I was being directed to turn on a road that didn't exist. I scrambled to correct my course, dragging both vehicles across multiple lanes of traffic to catch the freeway entrance. In my nervous confusion, I didn't realize until it was too late that I was entering a toll road. To make matters worse, I discovered I was headed east instead of west. Then I missed the exit where I could turn around. Swearing a blue streak, I drove mile after long mile out of my way to the next exit, racking up charges as I went.

This was in the days before electronic tolls were common and the toll booths were unmanned, requiring that the money be deposited into a steel container while you drove through.

I rummaged through my purse for every last bit of change I could scrape together, and still I came up short of the required toll. I dumped my change into the container and looked around for someone to tell me what to do if I didn't have enough money to pay the toll. No one was around and I saw no helpful instructions posted, so I pressed my foot on the gas pedal and drove through. I expected to see red flashing lights or hear a warning bell or siren, but nothing happened. I continued on, checking behind me every few miles for flashing lights, but none appeared. I exhaled and began to relax.

I made my way across the rest of Oklahoma and New Mexico without any more trouble and finally arrived in the high-desert city of Albuquerque. The rusty-colored Sandia Mountains cupped the east side of the city, while the sandy Rio Grande meandered south through the middle, eventually making its way to Texas.

The Albuquerque International Balloon Fiesta is an annual event and the largest hot-air balloon festival in the world. Hundreds of balloons participate in the event, which spans nine days. This was my first balloon festival and my first RV group event, and I had no idea what to expect.

I followed the signs directing me to the RV parking, as well as the directions I'd received from Cindy, who'd arrived before me. The RV parking was not an RV campground, but rather a dirt and gravel space that looked like a gigantic RV sales lot. Motorhomes and trailers of all types and sizes were parked in even, orderly rows. Cindy told me where she and her friends were parked, so I slowly made my way to the designated spot, recognizing the familiar retro look and colorful stripes of the motorhomes. I quickly parked the Green Monster, then unhooked the car from the tow bar. I pulled the car up close to the motorhome, as instructed by the parking attendants. Then, remembering what one of the instructors from Life on Wheels had told us, I climbed back into the driver's seat.

"RVs need to be parked reasonably level because of the refrigerator," the instructor told the class. "They work differently than the ones in our homes, and in order to keep the inner workings flowing properly, the refrigerator needs to be level. That means you will need some kind of levelers. Many RVs come with automatic levelers, which are like steel legs mounted on the underside of the RV that can be raised and lowered at the push of a button. The drawbacks with automatic levelers are that they are heavy and expensive. If you don't have automatic levelers, you'll need to get leveling blocks or use some other method to make sure the motorhome is level when parked."

I didn't have automatic levelers installed on my motorhome. Instead, I'd bought leveling blocks. They consisted of several sets of yellow plastic squares not much wider than the motorhome wheels that could be stacked to create flat-topped pyramids of varying height and steepness, which you drove on to raise the wheels. It was like driving onto a giant pile of Lego blocks. They were much trickier to use than automatic levelers. Figuring out how many blocks were needed for each wheel to make the motorhome level presented me with a new challenge. Then centering the wheels on the blocks took focus—especially for a newbie like me. Pressing too hard or softly on the gas pedal could result in the wheels' being either too far over the blocks or not far enough. Sometimes, they were too far to the left or too far to the right. I'd used the leveling blocks at my parents' house, so this was not my first time using them, but I was still learning this new skill.

When I got the motorhome I'd installed two small levels on the dashboard and driver's-side door of the Green Monster to tell me when it was level. I also placed a larger one in the middle of the motorhome floor by the refrigerator after I got parked. All of the levels now told me the motorhome was tilting.

I found my leveling blocks in the outside storage bin, put some of them under the front tires, and drove onto them, feeling satisfied when the bubbles in the levels were in the "level" zone. I felt pretty pleased with myself. I'd survived driving a thirty-foot motorhome—towing a car—through five states in three days without any major mishaps. *I can do this!*

As soon as I parked, Rylie emerged from beneath the passenger seat, as usual. "Ready for a walk, Rylie?" He wagged his tail as I snapped on his leash and we set out to find Cindy. I had talked with Cindy on the phone many times since we met in Tucson, so I felt like I was meeting a good friend. I found her red-striped motorhome, a twenty-six-footer, and knocked on the door.

"You made it!" Cindy's eyes twinkled when she saw me at the door.

"Thanks to your directions. I just got parked and I'm taking Rylie for a walk. Do you and Mona want to go with us?" Mona was Cindy's seventeen-year-old dog, a beagle and miniature pinscher mix.

"Sure, let me grab her leash." Cindy returned with Mona a moment later, and after Rylie and Mona got acquainted, we walked around the RV area. Cindy introduced me to some of the other group members, and we continued on our walk. She pointed out the "RV store," which was a tent stocked with Camping World items for sale.

We wandered over to the balloon-launch field, an enormous grassy area where the balloon crews were hard at work. We watched as they backed up their trucks, unloaded the gear, and unfolded the huge balloons, spreading them out on the grass. The baskets were hauled out of the backs of trucks and connected to the balloons, and then the propane tanks were used to start filling the balloons with hot air. It looked like a lot of hard but well-organized work. Once the balloons were filled, they stood upright and were ready for flight.

Not far from the launch field was an area filled with vendors selling everything from food to balloon paraphernalia. After touring the grounds and the vendor booths and catching up for a bit, Cindy and I agreed to meet up later. I could return to my motorhome and settle in. As I walked toward my parking spot, I noticed a small group of people whispering among themselves and occasionally shooting frowns in the direction of the Green Monster. As I approached, one of them came over to talk to me. It was Barry, one of the group members I'd met earlier.

Barry was in his sixties with a small, wiry frame and a serious expression. He moderated a website for motorhome owners and frequently handed out advice to people who posted questions. This website was a popular place to receive helpful responses from other members of the group. During my months of preparation before I hit the road, I'd spent hours scouring the posts, soaking up whatever knowledge I could. Questions about repairs and upgrades were plentiful, and more rarely, there were discussions about places to go. I'd even posted some questions myself and received a lot of help from the other members of the group.

Barry was pretty strict about the types of information that could be posted and seemed a stickler for doing repairs and upgrades correctly, without "damaging the integrity" of the motorhome or any of its components.

The grave look on Barry's face as he approached me sent my smile south, and I figured I must have done something terribly wrong. He pointed to the wheels of my motorhome, which were perched atop the leveling blocks.

"It's bad for the tires if they're hanging over the sides of the leveling blocks like that," Barry said. "I'm sure you don't want to ruin your brand-new tires."

I looked at my wheels. They were not directly centered on the leveling blocks, but it wasn't as though half the tire was hanging over the side. There was just the slightest bit of overhang. *Is this guy serious? Is that what everyone was whispering about? Do they scrutinize everyone's tires as closely as mine?* I felt like a naughty child who had just thrown a basketball in the living room and knocked over a treasured lamp. I was surprised this slight bit of tire overhang was enough to cause such a reaction in the group. These travelers took their motorhome care very seriously—and the care of other people's motorhomes, too.

"Oh, okay. Thanks," I said. "I'll try again."

I climbed into the cab with flushed cheeks and, with several people from the group directing me, backed the motorhome off the levelers, then drove up onto them again— but too far. The group motioned for me to back up, so I tried again. And again. My skin began to prickle with heat. After lurching to and fro a few times, I finally got all four tires centered on the blocks to the satisfaction of the group. They seemed to breathe a collective sigh of relief. Motorhome disaster averted. I wiped the perspiration from my upper lip, got out of the cab, thanked everyone for their help, and slunk into my motorhome. *This might be more of a challenge than I thought.*

CHAPTER 4

TAKING FLIGHT

OCTOBER 2006

There's something just magical about flight.

—Graham Hawkes

E arly the next morning, I woke up to a loud gasping noise. Rylie growled at the unfamiliar sound. It seemed to be coming from different directions outside the motorhome. While lying in bed, I raised the shade on the wide window at the head of it. My eyes looked skyward and widened.

Hundreds of hot-air balloons drifted into the post-dawn light, their bright colors and varied shapes filling the sky. Except for the occasional noise from the propane burners forcing hot air into the balloons, they glided silently up and away, chasing the rising sun. This huge balloon launch, known as the mass ascension, was an incredible spectacle. I watched with amazement as a pig floated by, surrounded by a bull, a bear, and a witch. A moment later a stagecoach chased a couple of bumblebees, while a genie on a magic carpet joined the crowd.

As I lay in bed watching this unusual scene floating past my window, I was consumed by an unfamiliar emotion: joy. I thought back to when I was envying the homeless people as I walked to the office. If my tilted mind had not envied the "freedom" of the homeless, I probably wouldn't have been here. A huge smile plastered my face as I scrambled to get my clothes on and go outside.

Some of my fellow campers were gathered nearby watching the show, including Cindy. When she saw me, she walked over to where I was standing, gawking at the sky.

"It's like daytime fireworks," she said.

"This is even better," I replied. "They don't disappear in a few seconds like fireworks."

Some of our neighbors climbed onto the roofs of their motorhomes to get a better view. Everyone craned their neck to watch the balloons fly unfettered into the sky. The sound of furiously clicking cameras mingled with the oohs and aahs of the crowd.

"Thanks for inviting me to join you here," I said to Cindy. "This is the perfect start to my new life. I think I'm taking flight, just like these balloons."

"Me too." She grinned.

The rest of the day was filled with various balloon activities, wandering the booths across the street from the RV parking lot, and meeting new friends. We gathered throughout the day and evening at the fiesta events and in small groups in each other's motorhomes to share stories, food, and wine.

As I got to know some of the other women parked near me, I was impressed with how confident and adventurous they were. Lucy had a generous figure with a helmet of thick gray hair, pixie features, and a gigantic smile that lit up her entire face. Her boisterous laugh and quick wit made her an instant friend with nearly everyone she met. During one of our conversations she told me she was divorced and lived full-time in her motorhome. Annie was a soft-spoken, slender woman in her early sixties with short, stylish hair; librarian glasses; and a hint of a Southern drawl. Annie told me she and Lucy had become friends years ago and often traveled together with their motorhomes.

The women came from a variety of circumstances. Some, like Lucy, traveled full-time, and others kept homes somewhere and traveled when they could sneak away for a few days or weeks. Some women were traveling without their husbands.

"I told my husband if he didn't want to go to the balloon fiesta, I was going anyway," one woman said. "So I did."

These women capably managed their motorhomes and were fluent in the language of tire pressure, tank dumping, and engine maintenance. I admired their independence and knowledge and wanted to be as confident managing my motorhome as they were.

One thing became very clear to me: the motorhome was an important focal point to this group. I watched and listened as they spent hours sharing stories, providing tours of the upgrades they'd made to their motorhomes, and discussing maintenance in great detail. After my experience with the leveling blocks, I could see that I wasn't taking my motorhome care as seriously as the rest of the group. I wasn't interested in doing any upgrades. The Green Monster had just gobbled up a large portion of my house sale profits, and I was only planning to travel full-time for a year, anyway. I toured the motorhome upgrades and aftermarket gadgets with the rest of the group, just enjoying getting to know everyone better. This kind of close-knit community had been missing from my life for a long time.

Activities at the balloon fiesta were highly dependent upon the weather. Rain or wind could cancel events. When we learned the program the following day would be canceled because of wind, Annie organized a group hike to Kasha-Katuwe Tent Rocks National Monument. Since dogs weren't allowed, Rylie would stay in the motorhome, but I wouldn't be gone long.

Volcanic explosions millions of years ago created unusual rock formations that looked like tents, or teepees, in a canyon. Eight of us piled into Annie's twenty-three-foot motorhome and made the one-hour drive north of Albuquerque. After getting parked, we gathered at the trailhead for a group photo, then started up the trail.

I gravitated toward Cindy because I remembered how some members of the group seemed so disapproving of the way I parked on my leveling blocks. There had been no judgment with Cindy, and she made me laugh. She was the only other person in the group near my age.

As we were skirting the rocks and boulders during our climb up the narrow canyon, I heard a groan from Cindy, who was behind me. I turned around to see her stopped on the trail. Her round face was rosy red, and she was breathing heavily.

"I got a twinge in my ankle," she said. "You go on ahead."

"Are you sure you're okay?" I asked. "I can stay here with you."

"No," Cindy said. "I just need a break, this is a steep climb. You should finish the hike. The view from the top is supposed to be incredible. I'll be right here when you come back down."

I reluctantly continued hiking, and soon found myself next to Annie.

"Where are you from, Annie?" I asked, noting her Southern accent.

"I live in Philadelphia now, but I grew up in New Orleans. I never completely lost the accent." We fell into easy conversation as we continued our climb up the canyon.

"Are you retired?" I asked.

"Yes, I retired from teaching a couple of years ago. Third grade."

"Lucky you! I wish I could retire and be a permanent full-timer. I'm just taking a year off to travel."

"Oh, I'm not a full-timer. I usually just travel for a few weeks at a time. I don't want to be away from my grandkids longer than that. Besides, I like having a house to return to. I get claustrophobic living in the motorhome for more than a month or two." Annie's motorhome was seven feet shorter than mine.

Some of the people I met, like Annie, were not interested in full-time travel, and had the financial resources to keep a house and leave for long periods in their RVs. Some, like me, couldn't afford the RV life unless they sold their homes. Others could afford to have a house but chose not to, because they didn't want to be tied down with the maintenance a house required and preferred the freedom of full-timing.

"What are some of your favorite places you've seen?" I asked.

As Annie talked in her soft-spoken way about some of her previous trips, my self-protective shell softened.

"Hiking is a good way to get to know people," Annie observed.

"I like connecting with people this way," I agreed. "I'm more comfortable talking with one or two people at a time instead of a large group."

When we reached the top of the canyon, we were rewarded for our efforts. The peaks of the tent rocks looked like gray, pointed toadstools scattered beneath us, and the distant Sandia Mountains shimmered in the sunlight like glowing coals. We took photos and enjoyed the view while eating a snack before heading back down the canyon.

During the return hike, I talked with some of the others in the group. They were easygoing and friendly, not rigid and judgmental as I'd thought at first. *Maybe I have more in common with this group than I thought.* Travel was a shared interest, but hiking, nature, and animals, too. Maybe they hadn't been trying to embarrass the newbie when they gathered around my motorhome to tell me about my poor parking job on the leveling blocks.

As we approached the bottom of the canyon, Cindy was waiting right where we left her.

"Are you feeling better?" I asked.

"Much better. I enjoyed just sitting here relaxing. I watched you all going up the canyon."

I felt relaxed too, and happier. This square peg was feeling rounder, but there were more lessons to learn on this journey to self-confidence.

The next day a group of us were gathered near our RVs, chatting after the mass ascension.

"Catch them!" yelled a panicked voice.

We looked toward the voice, across the row of RVs parked next to ours. We saw a woman running after two brown, anxious-looking dachshunds headed our way, barking wildly. It was surprising how quickly they could move on their stubby legs.

One of the women in our group reached down to grab a dog and was promptly bitten by the clearly hysterical creature. I stood nearby with Rylie on his leash, and the dog ran straight for me, desperately trying to climb up my leg with a frenzied set of leaps. I wanted to pick the dog up, but before I could do anything the petrified pooch stopped jumping and instead started relieving itself where it stood—on my shoe. While I leaped out of the way, the woman chasing the dogs finally caught up and snapped a leash on the dog's collar. This immediately seemed to calm the dog down, and when the other dachshund came over, he was quickly leashed.

"Your dogs seemed pretty excited," said Arlene, one of the group members.

"They aren't mine, they belong to the guy in the trailer next to me. He had a heart attack and they were stuck in there with him for a long time. Another neighbor went to check on him after hearing the dogs barking like crazy, found him on the floor, and called an ambulance. I'm just taking them out for a walk to help, but the poor dogs are scared out of their wits."

Although I was in my forties and healthy, this experience shook me. It dawned on me that there were all kinds of things that could go wrong when traveling alone. Feeling a mad rush of fear, I became a hysterical dachshund in my thoughts, chasing my tail into a needless frenzy of worry. *What if I become dangerously sick or fall unconscious? What if I drop dead of a heart attack or a brain aneurysm? What would happen to Rylie, left alone in the motorhome? How would Cammie and the rest of my family know what happened to me? How long would it take someone to realize something was wrong? What if a tire blew out on the freeway and caused a horrible accident? What if I fell and hurt myself on one of my solo hikes, or the motorhome broke down on some deserted highway, right in the path of a serial killer? No wonder people keep telling me how brave I am—all kinds of things could go wrong!* My thoughts crashed around from one disaster to the next like a moth in a lampshade, becoming increasingly irrational.

"Do you ever worry about what might happen when you're traveling alone?" I asked Cindy, who was standing next to me.

"I thought about it at first, but then I realized that I'm not any more alone in my motorhome than I was when I lived in my house. Something could have happened to me just as easily when I was living there. I could have fallen off a ladder when I was painting or slipped and hit my head in the shower. Things can happen anywhere."

"That's true," I agreed. "I had to climb onto the roof once to clear the branches after a windstorm using a rickety ladder. I could have fallen off and ended up unconscious in the yard. It probably would have taken one of my neighbors even longer to notice that something was wrong, because we hardly ever saw each other."

"That's right. Since I've been traveling, I meet and talk to people every day. Whether it's other travelers, campground owners, or friends, I've been in regular contact with someone, and that didn't always happen in my condo. Travelers are usually friendly and helpful. They look out for each other."

"I've seen a bit of that already," I said. "The guy who had the heart attack and his poor dogs were discovered by his neighbors before anything really bad happened."

Cindy was quiet for a moment, then said, "I've spent too much time obsessing about my brain tumor or worrying about something that might happen in the future. I decided that's a waste of time, so I'm not doing that anymore. I'm going to live my dream instead."

"Me too," I replied. *Feel the fear and take the leap anyway. My new motto.* I put the hysterical dachshunds out of my mind and went off to clean my shoes.

CHAPTER 5

TRAVELING COMPANIONS

OCTOBER-NOVEMBER 2006

It's never too late in life to have a genuine adventure.

—Robert Kurson

"Hey, do you want to go see the rest of the state?" Cindy asked when the balloon fiesta was over.

I didn't hesitate. "Sure, let's go." Other than seeing the country, I had no plan for what I would do after the balloon fiesta.

"I heard that Navajo Lake State Park is pretty, and there are pueblo ruins nearby. We could start there."

"Sounds like a plan. Let's do it." I liked this new lifestyle of spur-of-the-moment decisions.

When we told our circle of new friends at the balloon fiesta where we were headed, Theresa and Sarah wanted to join us. Both Theresa and Sarah were in their late fifties, and neither was retired. Theresa's long, gray-brown hair framed her piercing blue eyes, and her black lab mix was well behaved. She chattered practically nonstop, while the rest of us struggled to squeeze in a word now and then. Sarah was petite and slender, with short black hair. She was the opposite of Theresa, quiet and reserved. Both women had husbands waiting for them back home.

41

Lucy and Annie said they would meet up with us later on, so we got our caravan in order, pointed our motorhome noses north, and hit the highway. Before long, we were crossing the Continental Divide as we headed toward the state's northern border.

Navajo Lake State Park sat right at the New Mexico-Colorado border and included a dam, which could be driven upon by way of a very narrow dirt road, barely wide enough for two cars. The dam was in a seldom-traveled, rural area typical of much of New Mexico. It was the kind of place where if you got in a bind, there might not have been help any time soon, so I was grateful for my traveling companions. There were no barriers on either side of the dam road to prevent vehicles from tumbling down the steep embankment and into the water. We found ourselves mistakenly headed there as we struggled to find the campground.

"We're heading the wrong way. We need to turn around." This was Cindy, who was leading our caravan, on the CB radio.

The other three women were driving shorter motorhomes, and none of them was towing a car. They were easily able to do a U-turn in an intersection of the dam road. Then it was my turn. This was the first time I was attempting such a maneuver. Remembering that I couldn't back up with the car attached, I made the turn as wide as I could. Although I was pulling hard on the steering wheel, it was like trying to turn around a cruise ship in a tiny stream. As the Green Monster's wheels inched dangerously close to the edge of the dam road, my eyes slid down the steep bank toward the water far below, my heart pounding. *Am I going to make it?* I crawled a tiny bit further. *I'm not going to make it!*

I realized too late that I couldn't stop and unhook the car, because I was turning in such a tight circle. Tight angles locked up the tow bar and made it impossible to release it and unhook the car. To make matters worse, I saw that if I didn't topple over the side of the dam, I was headed toward what appeared to be a very large pothole on the side of the road. It was filled with water, so I couldn't tell how deep it was. I aimed for the puddle anyway. I cranked the steering wheel with every bit of strength I had, barely keeping the motorhome on the top of the dam, and just missing the pothole. *I made it!*

"Nice!" Cindy said over the radio. "I wasn't sure you were going to make it." She had pulled over to the side of the road to wait for me.

"Remind me not to do that again," I responded weakly, my hand shaking as it held the radio. *Note to self: No U-turns in tight spots with the car attached.* I was learning.

By the time we found the campground, my heart rate had returned to normal. We all got settled into tree-studded campsites with beautiful views of the lake. This was going to be base camp while we saw the sights nearby.

Since I was the only one with a car, we all piled into my Honda for our daily field trips after we got our dogs walked, fed, and settled down for their naps in their respective motorhomes. Our first visit was to Aztec Ruins National Monument, where the ancestral Pueblo people built elaborate stone structures between 1100 and 1300 AD. We wandered around the mostly deserted self-guided trail among the crumbling brick dwellings and kivas, which are ceremonial structures. Theresa kept up a steady stream of chatter throughout the day and evening, while the rest of us listened politely, occasionally trying to squeeze in a few words. The next day, we took my car across the Colorado border to visit Mesa Verde National Park.

Mesa Verde contained six hundred cliff dwellings of the Pueblo people, including some of the best-preserved sites in the country. Sandstone, mortar, and wood-beam structures dating as far back as 1190 AD were tucked beneath overhanging cliffs as though under great protective wings. We followed our ranger guide on foot along the dusty trails and marveled at the many yellow and salmon-colored rooms of Cliff Palace and Balcony House. Throughout our tour, I marveled at Theresa's ability to talk nonstop without seeming to take a breath or allow a pause for others to interject some conversation. *She must say every thought that comes into her head.*

Our last foray was to Chaco Culture National Historical Park in New Mexico, but instead of taking my car, we each drove our motorhome for this trip. We planned to go our separate ways afterward. Getting there required bumping along a pothole-filled dirt road, which we were told became flooded and impassable during rainy weather. We kept an eye on the gathering rain clouds while we made our plans. We arranged to meet Lucy and Annie there, and after a couple of cell phone calls to coordinate meeting places and times, we finally found them and started driving the nine-mile loop to see the ruins.

These Pueblo structures were older, going back as far as 850 AD, and were not as well preserved as those in Mesa Verde. Huge rocks lit up like fireballs by the sun lined the canyon on either side, with green mesquite bushes polka-dotting the canyon floor between them. Theresa's never-ending chatter began grinding on my nerves. I knew I was quieter than most, so I figured I was the only one bothered by the nonstop monologue. When we were photographing the many brick doorways lined up inside Pueblo Bonito, Cindy wandered away from the group and I followed.

"Doesn't she ever shut up?" Cindy asked when we were safely out of earshot. "She talks more than I can listen."

"I thought I was the only one slowly going mad," I replied, and we both dissolved into giggles. This life of freedom and travel wasn't without small annoyances, and it was time to move on. Not everyone is an ideal traveling companion.

Since Theresa was returning to work, and Sarah only had a few days before her planned return to her husband, we knew we were parting ways after Chaco Canyon. I admired Theresa and Sarah for not letting their husbands' lack of enthusiasm about travel keep them from pursuing what they loved. Lucy, Annie, Cindy, and I were all headed back to Albuquerque, so goodbyes and hugs were passed around, and a trail of dust and occasional raindrops followed each motorhome as we all drove the long, lonely road out of the canyon. I enjoyed the silence as I drove back to Albuquerque.

The four of us decided to stay at the Coronado State Monument campground near Albuquerque so we could see some more of the city. One evening Lucy, Annie, Cindy, and I were sitting in the campground outside our motorhomes watching a blood-red sunset paint the nighttime sky.

"Some friends of mine are going to the Baja Peninsula," Lucy said. "They spend a few months every winter on a beach in the middle of the peninsula and said it's really beautiful. It's also really cheap living. I'm thinking about going too."

"Really?" Annie asked. "I'd like to go."

"That sounds like fun," Cindy chimed in. "I want to go too!" They both turned to me expectantly.

I looked around our little group. I had become really fond of these women, even though we hadn't known each other very long. "Sure, I'm game," I said. "When are we going?" I was learning to just go with the flow, seizing whatever opportunity life brought my way, not worrying about the future. *Now, this is freedom!*

We checked calendars and decided we would all meet in San Diego toward the end of January and cross the border together on February first. With our plans made, Annie and Lucy decided to explore more of the western part of New Mexico, while Cindy and I wanted to see the eastern and southern part of the state. We agreed to meet up again at Rockhound State Park in the southwest in a couple of weeks.

Cindy and I visited national parks and monuments, including White Sands and Carlsbad Caverns, which couldn't have been more different. White Sands was an albino gypsum desert under a brilliant blue sky, and the spooky corners of the craggy caverns were a great setting for a murder. Thousands of bats roosted near the natural entrance to the caves, but we weren't there at the right time of year to see them. I loved exploring all of these uniquely different sights, and Cindy was a great traveling companion: she was easygoing, capable, curious, and didn't talk nonstop. I also learned a lot from her.

One day she knocked on my door and said, "I'm going to change the oil on my generator. Do you want to watch to see how it's done?"

Normally, that was something I would pay someone to do for me, but I knew I needed to take a more active role in my motorhome care. "Yes, I do. I'll be right there."

"That's easier than I thought it would be," I said as I watched Cindy drain the oil from her generator into a plastic container.

"The tricky part is figuring out which campgrounds will let you do motorhome maintenance," Cindy replied. "Some of them don't allow it."

"Good to know. I wouldn't have thought of that." Although it seemed I had learned so much already, I was still learning.

Another time we were sitting in my motorhome with the roof vents open when it started to rain. Big drops splashed through the screen into my living room as I scrambled to crank the vents shut.

"I got vent covers for my motorhome and installed them myself. Now I can leave the vents open when it's raining and still get some fresh air without getting the motorhome all wet inside. They make the plastic vents last longer, too."

"That makes sense. I'll have to get some of those." It sounded like a good idea. The next time we were at an RV supply store, I bought some vent covers. Cindy climbed up onto the roof with me and told me how to drill the holes with my new drill and install the covers myself. I eyed my handiwork and felt the little seed of my self-confidence grow larger.

We got along well, but it was in Santa Fe that I learned what a great friend Cindy was. We'd been visiting Taos, a popular skiing destination with a quaint town square at the foot of the gorgeous Sangre de Cristo Mountains. We toured the pueblo and an art gallery, then ate dinner in one of the restaurants in town. It was early November, the temperatures were dropping, and Taos is at eight thousand feet elevation. When we woke up the next morning to find our water hoses on the motorhomes partially frozen, we decided it was time to move to a lower elevation.

I wasn't feeling well when I woke up, and by the time we made the hour-and-a-half drive to Santa Fe, I knew I was sick. I got the motorhome parked in Santa Fe and fell into bed.

When Cindy knocked on my door to go explore the town, she took one look at my ghostly pale face and said, "What's wrong?"

"I'm sick. I think I ate something bad. I'm sorry, I can't go anywhere."

"Don't worry about me," Cindy said. "Just take care of yourself. I'll walk Rylie for you before I go exploring." With that she snapped on Rylie's leash and took him outside. I crawled back into bed and immediately fell asleep. I woke up when Cindy returned with Rylie a short time later. "I filled up his food and water dishes so he's all set."

"Thank you," I said faintly from my nest in the covers. I spent the rest of the day shuffling between the bed and the bathroom. Luckily, they weren't far apart. As promised, Cindy returned late in the afternoon and walked and fed Rylie again. I slept through the night and when I woke up the next morning, I felt better. I remembered what one of my fellow travelers had told me. *Travelers look out for each other.* I was so grateful to have Cindy's companionship when I needed help.

CHAPTER 6

DEATH ON THE TRAIL

NOVEMBER 2006

*It is not death that man should fear, but he should fear
never beginning to live.*

—Marcus Aurelius

C indy and I each bought an annual New Mexico state park
pass when we left Albuquerque, which allowed very low-
cost camping in any of the parks. We took advantage of this,
sampling a good portion of the campgrounds in the state
system. Although a few of them had lakes, they weren't the
pretty, tree-rimmed lakes I grew up with in Minnesota or
camped near in California. This was high-desert country, and
trees were sparse, but I was trying to adjust to the scenery.
Eventually, we made our way to Rockhound State Park to meet
up with Lucy and Annie.

Rockhound is located in the Little Florida Mountains, not
far from Deming. It got its name from the abundance of
minerals in the area, which attracts visitors in search of quartz
crystals, jasper, perlite, and other minerals. When I first drove
into the park, my face fell. The area was covered in desert scrub
and cactus. It looked parched and uninviting. My eyes couldn't
latch onto anything of interest here. Not only were there no trees,

but there weren't even any tall bushes like we'd seen in some of the other state parks. All of the campsites were completely exposed and baking in the sun, which hammered against my innate need for cover and privacy. I grew up in the trees and always feel most at home when I am surrounded by tall, leafy protection. The stark desert landscape felt completely foreign to me, and it was unsettling. I felt exposed and vulnerable. The only interesting sight was a wall of rock formations high atop the nearby hill, and I decided I would hike up there once I got settled in. But I would soon change my mind.

Lucy and Annie were already at the campground when we arrived. Cindy and I spent some time getting settled into our respective campsites and chatting with Lucy and Annie. After we got caught up, I said, "I think I'll go for a hike up the hill. Does anyone want to join me?"

"I don't hike," Lucy said.

"I would, except I hurt my foot and need to take it easy for a few days," Annie said.

"It's too hot for me," Cindy said.

"Okay, why don't we meet up later for happy hour?" I suggested. Everyone agreed. I went into my motorhome to change into my hiking clothes. I opened the drawers beneath the bed and took out my socks and sports bra, and put them on the bed, where Rylie was lounging. Then I went to the closet on the other side of the bed and got a pair of shorts and a T-shirt. When I turned around, I took one look at Rylie and burst out laughing. In a matter of seconds, Rylie had somehow managed to get my sports bra over his head.

"Are you getting dressed, too, Rylie?" I grabbed my camera and snapped a photo. He looked embarrassed. I removed the bra from his head, changed my clothes, grabbed his leash, and headed outside for a hike.

When we emerged from the motorhome, I saw a dust trail plowing along the entrance road to the park. I watched as several sheriff's deputy vehicles sped along the dirt road and parked next to the camp host's motorhome. The camp host or hosts, if a couple, are the on-site managers of the campground, usually staying in a motorhome or trailer. I walked over to where Lucy, Cindy, and Annie were sitting in camp chairs outside Lucy's motorhome. "What do you suppose that's about?" I asked them.

"No clue," said Cindy. We watched as the camp host emerged from his RV and spoke with the deputies for some time, pointing to the rocky hill nearby. Before long, we saw more vehicles arrive and a handful of people with "CSI" printed on their shirts climbing up and down the hill and disappearing around the bend when they were near the top.

"I guess I'm not going to hike that hill," I said.

"It's not looking good," Lucy agreed.

Eventually, our curiosity got the better of us, so we wandered over to one of our neighbors, Bill, and asked if he knew what was going on.

"They found a dead body up behind those rocks on the hill," Bill said, pointing to the area where I'd planned to hike. "They think she was a hiker, and they're treating it as a crime scene."

This was sobering news. *If they're treating the area as a crime scene, doesn't that mean they think she was murdered?* All sorts of questions started zipping through my mind, with no one to provide answers. *Is this a dangerous area, or was this just a fluke? Who was this woman, and who killed her? More importantly, where is the killer?*

Although I had been traveling with others since I arrived in New Mexico, I realized that soon I would be on my own. The dead woman was an example of the dangers that could befall a woman traveling alone. I wanted to explore the sights not just on wheels, but also on foot. Since many of the national parks and some state parks didn't allow dogs on the trails, I couldn't always have Rylie with me. That meant I would be hiking alone. *Is it safe for me to hike on my own?* I felt uneasy, but hikers always seemed so friendly and good-natured, it was hard to imagine a hiker being a killer.

"Do you carry a gun?" Bill asked.

I had been asked several times while traveling if I carried a gun or some other weapon. I didn't. I had never fired a gun in my life and wasn't about to start.

"No, I don't. I think there are too many guns in our country as it is, and they aren't making us any safer."

"Do you have pepper spray?"

"Nope," I replied with a smile. "I have this ferocious attack dog." Bill looked at mild-mannered, twenty-five-pound Rylie and laughed.

I remembered when I was at Life on Wheels and attended a class for solo travelers. We were given information about various groups that catered to the solo traveler, but safety information was also discussed. One woman in the class said she had been traveling on her own for a long time.

"I don't have a dog, but I have a pair of beat-up men's work boots in a very large size. As soon as I get settled into a new campsite, I put the boots outside my door so that people will think I have a really large husband inside my RV. I've never had any trouble."

Rylie was fairly small but he had a big bark. I decided to play that up and bought a very large dog dish the next day when I was in town. It was the size a Great Dane or Doberman might have. I showed it to Rylie.

"What do you think, Rylie? Does this bring out your inner Doberman?" He looked at me with a quizzical expression and gave the dish a sniff. From then on, I always put it right outside the door of my motorhome on my colorful camping mat when I got settled in a new campsite. I also attached a long leash to the outside door handle, so it was clear there was a dog nearby.

Someone up to no good might think twice about coming close to the motorhome if they saw that, and Rylie always barked when someone was near.

Six weeks had passed since I started touring New Mexico with my new friends, and it was time for us to go our separate ways. Cindy was headed back to Southern California for a medical checkup, Annie was returning to Philadelphia, Lucy was meeting up with her son, and I would explore Arizona on my own before heading back to California to see Cammie for Christmas. Although I was sad to part with these fun women, I was looking forward to meeting up with them again when we traveled down the Baja Peninsula in a couple of months. We never did learn the outcome of the murder investigation, but I soon pushed it out of my mind.

CHAPTER 7

HOLIDAYS

NOVEMBER 2006-JANUARY 2007

Maybe you had to leave in order to really miss a place;
maybe you had to travel to figure out how beloved your
starting point was.

—*Jodi Picoult*

"I can't go with you to Baja." Cindy's voice on the phone sounded flat and resigned. "A big birthday party is being planned for my grandma's ninetieth birthday, and I have to be here for it."

I swallowed a lead ball of disappointment. "Of course, you have to be there for your grandma's birthday party. I understand." Part of me understood, because I wished that I had been able to celebrate my grandma's ninetieth birthday with her, but she didn't live that long. The other part of me—the childish part—wanted to say, *"But you promised!"* I had really been counting on Cindy's going on the trip to Baja. I kept the childish thoughts to myself. "We'll miss you, but maybe we can all go to Baja again sometime."

After we said goodbye and ended the call, my disappointment returned. I realized how much I'd relied on Cindy's companionship while I was traveling in New Mexico. Of all the people that I'd met during my short time on the road, I felt I had the most in common with Cindy. She was near my own age, single, and not yet ready to retire. We'd connected immediately when we met at Life on Wheels. She was also very outgoing, which meant it was easier for me to meet people when I was with her. I didn't know Lucy and Annie as well, because I hadn't spent as much time with them.

A week later, more bad news arrived, this time in an email. Annie's aunt had passed away, and she needed to tend to her affairs. She would not be going to Baja, either. I felt sad for Annie and sent her my sympathies. I understood completely, but my distress deepened. Next to Cindy, I had connected with Annie most easily because of the time we spent hiking together. A couple of days later, I received another email, this time from Lucy. Since Cindy and Annie had canceled, she had asked her friends Karen and Elaine, whom I'd met at the balloon fiesta, to join the Baja caravan.

If I wanted to go to Baja as planned, I would be traveling with Lucy, Karen, and Elaine. I'd only spent a short time talking with Karen and Elaine at the balloon fiesta and barely knew them. All three were fifteen to twenty-five years older than me, retired, and experienced RVers, making me feel even more like an outsider. One of the reasons Cindy and I had bonded so quickly was that we were both new to RVing and on a similar learning curve, although Cindy had a few months' head start.

I began feeling a bit nervous about traveling thousands of miles and spending two months in another country with these three women. I knew after a few days with Theresa that not everyone was an ideal traveling companion. Although we would be in separate motorhomes, we would be spending a lot of time together, and would be making group decisions about where to go and what to do. If we didn't get along, two months in Baja would feel like an eternity.

My Spanish was extremely limited, and I had heard stories of crime in Mexico. I'd read about one couple camped in a remote area who were robbed at gunpoint. Others were pulled over by corrupt police officers for nonexistent traffic infractions and forced to pay them money to avoid being taken to jail. I decided it wasn't a good idea to travel there alone.

I wrestled with the decision of whether to go. *Should I continue with my plans and travel with these relative strangers? I really want to see the Baja Peninsula, but I have a bad feeling about going. Is it intuition or fear?* I was always getting the two confused. After agonizing over the decision for a few days, I remembered my new motto, "Feel the fear and take the leap anyway." *I'm going.* I hoped I was making the right decision.

Cammie was celebrating Thanksgiving with her boyfriend and his parents, so I spent the holiday alone, exploring the Tucson desert. This was the first time in my life I'd spent Thanksgiving by myself, but I didn't mind. I felt empowered traveling alone. Every morning, Rylie woke me up by lying on my chest and licking my face—much better than a shrieking alarm clock. "Good morning, Rylie," I mumbled, stroking the soft fur on the top of his head. I got dressed and snapped the leash on his collar, and we went out to explore Saguaro National Park. It was in this park that I first discovered the brittle beauty of the desert.

We followed the sandy, single-track trails, wandering among the saguaro soldiers of the park. This enormous cactus with arm-like appendages and thick, spiny skin was common in Arizona and especially plentiful in the park. I found something strangely comforting about them as we hiked, although we were careful to keep our distance from the sharp needles decorating them. The towering stick figures felt almost like companions next to the trails, interspersed here and there with prickly pear, ocotillo, and other succulents. The weather was sunny and warm, but not blistering, especially in the early morning.

When we returned from our walk I dumped some kibble and treats in Rylie's dish, gave him fresh water, then made my own breakfast. I took four steps from the kitchen to the small dining table to eat. I ate leisurely, smiling as I watched through the large motorhome windows as roadrunners scampered around the campground. I had never seen them before, and I was reminded of the cartoon from my childhood as I watched them sprinting on long legs with their Mohawk caps and bobbing tails. I breathed deeply, completely relaxed.

In mid-December, it was time to lumber back to California to visit Cammie for the Christmas holidays. After Rylie and I had one last walk in the park I washed the dishes, stowed everything away in the small cupboards, and folded the table into the cabinet. I lowered the TV antenna with a crank handle on the ceiling of the motorhome and made sure all cupboards and drawers were closed and the latches secured.

I went out to the side of the motorhome, turned off the campsite water, unscrewed the hose from the water spigot and the motorhome, coiled it up, and put it in one of the outside storage bins. Then I turned off the electricity, unplugged the electrical cord from both ends, and stowed it in the bin. I moved to the back of the Green Monster, got a pair of disposable gloves from the storage bin on the rear of the motorhome, put them on, and closed the valve on the sewer tank. I unhooked the sewer hose from the motorhome, holding it high in the air to let anything remaining in it drain into the campground sewer system, then packed the hose into a plastic storage bag inside a large plastic bin and put it in the motorhome. After peeling off my gloves and tossing them in the trash, I got my tire pressure gauge and checked the tire pressure in all six tires.

I climbed into the driver's seat and started the Green Monster's engine. I drove out of the campsite and parked the motorhome on the road next to it. Then I got out of the cab, walked over to where the car was parked, got in and started the car, and drove it right up behind the motorhome. With the engine in the car still running, I hooked the tow bar on the motorhome up to the car and plugged in the supplemental braking system, securing the safety cables to the underside of the motorhome. I returned to the car and put the car into each gear in order, then put the car in neutral and turned off the key. I climbed into the motorhome and turned on the back-up camera so I could keep an eye on the car while I was driving. With my lengthy departure routine complete, I was finally ready to hit the road.

RV camping was very scarce in the San Francisco Bay Area, but Cammie had a solution. "Ryan's parents said you can park the motorhome in their driveway."

Ryan's parents, Sue and David, lived in an East Bay suburban neighborhood where the homes were squeezed together like milk cartons in the dairy case. I pulled up in front of their well-kept house and unhooked my car. With David as my spotter, it took several nail-biting tries for me to back the Green Monster into the narrow driveway, carefully avoiding the fence on the left and the row of fresh petunias on the right. I made sure to position the door so that I wouldn't trample any flowers when I came out of the motorhome.

This was my first Christmas in the motorhome, and it felt so foreign, it was like being exiled in Siberia. It was bitterly cold by Bay Area standards, and the unusually frigid air seeped into the motorhome and into my very thoughts. I bundled up in my warmest clothes when I walked Rylie several times a day, but I felt out of place and out of sorts.

I hadn't expected this. Up until now, I had been happy with my new lifestyle. I'd experienced some occasional stress and brief fears or annoyances, but they usually disappeared pretty quickly. This was the first time I felt disillusioned with my new lifestyle. Parking in someone's driveway for Christmas was awkward. I felt like an imposition, and I missed my little house.

This feeling was amplified one day when I returned to the motorhome from running errands. As I drove up to Sue and David's house, I saw a police car parked in front of it. David was in the street, talking with the police officer. As I was parking my car, the policeman got in his patrol car and drove off.

"What was that about?" I asked David.

"Oh, that was just Crazy Carla, our neighbor, up to her usual nonsense. She's always complaining about something."

"What did she complain about?"

"She called the police to complain about the motorhome being parked in the driveway, but it's okay. Tim, the police officer, is a friend of mine and I explained that the motorhome is just here for a couple of weeks. Carla is always calling the cops about something, so this is nothing new. Nothing to worry about."

"But, David, I don't want to cause you and Sue any trouble with your neighbor. I can move the motorhome."

"No need for that," David said. "We've been having trouble with Carla for years—everyone in the neighborhood has. That's just Crazy Carla, and we're used to it. She'll get over it, she always does."

Knowing I'd upset a neighbor made me feel even more like a sore thumb, but David overruled my objections.

One day when Cammie was visiting me in the motorhome I told her, "I was missing having a Christmas tree, and all of the other holiday decorations I used to put in the house, so I bought this fake tree." I showed her the little tree I had decorated with tiny, doll-sized ornaments. I put it on the table, the only space in the motorhome large enough to hold even a tiny tree.

"It's cute," Cammie said, being generous.

"Really? You don't think it looks like a Charlie Brown Christmas tree? Well, it's the best I can do with the limited space in here." It wasn't just Christmas at my house that I was missing. I remembered how in the summertime the yard was decorated with lilacs, fruit trees, and roses. I felt a lump of sadness in my throat.

Recurring anxiety about my upcoming trip to the Baja Peninsula continued to plague me. *Why didn't I cancel when Cindy canceled? I have to go. The trip is only a month away.* In January, I spent time researching Baja and kept in touch with my caravan companions. Lucy, Karen, and Elaine passed on the helpful tidbits they learned about Baja and shared their enthusiasm for the upcoming trip. I couldn't find fault with anything they did, yet my apprehensions about going returned. *What am I afraid of?*

Then it dawned on me. *Fitting in.* I wasn't just worried about not getting along with my traveling companions. I was afraid of feeling like an outsider. I sometimes felt anxious in social situations with people I didn't know well. I liked to have my own transportation if I was going to a group event, so that I could escape if I needed to. This would be two months with strangers in a foreign country where I didn't speak the language, and where it apparently wasn't safe to travel alone. It sounded to me like a recipe for feeling like a square peg in a round hole. *This again. I am forty-five years old; when am I going to feel comfortable in my own skin?*

I flashed back to when I was twenty, when I would sometimes attend parties with friends. I would be having fun, then all of a sudden, I'd feel an overpowering need to get away from the crowd and be by myself. *I need quiet.* I would escape the chatter and slip outside unnoticed, regaining my bearings in the frosty stillness of a Minnesota winter. After a few minutes of quiet solitude, I would rejoin the party.

I'd spent most of my life feeling like an outsider, like I didn't fit in. While I was growing up, my dad's alcoholism was a constant presence, yet no one ever talked about it. The elephant in the room was never discussed. The clouds of unspoken words billowed around the constantly chattering television, a feeble attempt to disguise the emptiness. *The House of Silence.* We rarely had people over during my later childhood, or socialized much beyond extended family, so social events were unfamiliar territory for me. We acted like everything was fine, but I always knew that something wasn't right. My dad's alcoholism became a shameful secret. I felt like I was different from most of the other kids at school and I withdrew even further into my shy, quiet self. I just didn't fit in.

I was a senior in high school when my dad received yet another citation for driving while intoxicated, but this time he had to stay in jail at night and was only released during the day to work. I was finally old enough to name the elephant in the room. I approached my mom.

"Dad is an alcoholic," I told her. I felt an immense relief at finally speaking the truth that had been lurking in the corners all these years.

"Do you think so?" My mom looked doubtful. I didn't know if she was in denial or didn't want to talk about it. "He never drinks at home."

That was true; there was never a drop of alcohol in our house. I'm sure that was a big part of why my dad was rarely home. He was often at the bar near work where his friends hung out. My mom and I often stopped there on our way home from errands or shopping to coax him into coming home so he wouldn't drive drunk. Sometimes it worked.

My mom finally accepted the truth of my dad's alcoholism, although I think she must have known it all along. But nothing seemed to change. Anger began taking root deep inside me, branching beneath the surface, its tendrils curling around my bones and organs and seeping into my heart. We didn't express anger in the House of Silence, so I never learned how to deal with it in a healthy way. My parents treated each other with chilly quiet or avoidance when they were angry. Because my anger had nowhere to go, it festered into depression that quickly consumed me. During my senior year I started avoiding school, telling my mom I was sick. Because my grades were still good and I only needed a couple of credits to graduate, the school didn't do anything about it, other than give me extra homework assignments.

After graduating from high school, I decided I wanted out of the House of Silence. Instead of racking up a bunch of college debt and living at home, I got a job immediately after high school with Northwestern Bell, known back then as "the phone company," working in the business office. I moved into an apartment with a couple of friends as soon as I could afford it. I was starting my own life, unencumbered by my past. At least that's what I told myself, but of course, our past comes with us. My dad did finally quit drinking, but not until I was almost thirty and living in California.

But all of that was long ago. I was no longer a confused and lonely kid with a family secret. *I am a middle-aged woman who raised a child by myself and was successful enough to buy a house in California. I am traveling in an RV on my own, and I can fit in wherever I want.* Then I remembered how I'd felt watching the freedom of the homeless people while I was commuting to my old job in San Francisco. I gave myself a mental shake. *This is the life I wanted. I'm going to Baja, and I'm going to have fun!* I shoved my fears aside and prepared for Mexico.

I thirstily read blogs written by RV travelers in Baja and stocked up on books, maps, and spare parts for the motorhome. I saw a few online posts that said finding good parts for RVs in the remote areas of Baja was difficult. I guessed at what might come in handy based on the experiences and recommendations of others, and stuffed parts here and there into my petite storage compartments. I wanted to be prepared and confident for this trip.

Toward the end of January, it was time to say goodbye to Cammie and head south to San Diego to meet up with my Baja traveling companions.

"I don't know how often I'll be able to call, but I'll email as much as I can," I told Cammie. "I'll try Skype, too. I'm sure gonna miss you."

"I'll miss you too, but don't worry about me." Cammie gave me a big hug.

I climbed into the cab of the motorhome. "I love you," I called out the window, waving.

"Love you too, Mom. Remember to have fun!" Cammie said and waved as I drove off. Neither of us knew then what a life-changing experience my trip to Baja would be.

CHAPTER 8

BAJA

FEBRUARY 2007

*Good company in a journey makes the way
seem shorter.*

—Izaak Walton

"You made it," Lucy said as I stood outside the door of her motorhome. She wore her usual uniform of generous T-shirt, baggy shorts, Crocs, and a huge smile.

"*Hola.*" I grinned. "I'm ready for Baja." Although I'd been trying to learn Spanish, I couldn't remember more than a few words when I opened my mouth to speak.

Even after parking at our meeting place near the beach in San Diego, I still wasn't sure if I was making the right decision, but I was committed to going. After I walked the beach with Rylie and got reacquainted with my traveling companions for a few days, my gut started unclenching.

One evening we talked about what we wanted to do while we were in Baja.

"I want to meet up with my friends Frankie and Stan on El Coyote Beach," Lucy said.

"I want to see the whales," I added.

"I want to have a lobster dinner at a little place south of Tijuana that I visited when I was there ten years ago," Karen announced. "I have fond memories of that place."

"I want to relax on the beach as much as possible," Elaine said.

We decided that was enough planning. On February first, our four brightly striped motorhomes sailed across the border at San Ysidro with barely a glance from the Mexican border patrol. We stopped to get our tourist cards in Tijuana, then crept through a snaggletoothed traffic jam, desperately trying to exit the city.

Tijuana wore a cloak of grit and grime, and its roadsides were liberally peppered with trash. The cars were lined up bumper to bumper, barely crawling. We were anxious to see this crowded city in the rearview mirror, but the packed roads weren't cooperating. After getting lost a few times with each of the other ladies taking turns leading the caravan, my frustrated companions appointed me the leader, and I reluctantly took my turn. By sheer luck, I somehow found the way to Highway 1, otherwise known as the Baja Highway. This narrow two-lane road would eventually take us more than a thousand miles down the length of the peninsula. We slowly inched our way out of town.

The recently paved road had no shoulder, only a canyonlike drop off the pavement to dirt. I made a mental note to keep my wheels on the pavement. Before we crossed the border, we'd heard stories of RV travelers getting their driver's-side mirrors sheared off by passing semitrucks, so we folded in our mirrors. I turned on my back-up camera to tell me what was approaching from behind so I wasn't blind to passing traffic.

My research had told me months ago that I couldn't tow a vehicle in Baja with only one driver in my motorhome, so I wasn't towing my car. It was so much more comfortable, it was like going braless. *Driving the Green Monster is so easy now!*

Although I wished for my car a few times during my Baja journey, for the most part, I was so grateful that I didn't have to worry about it. Driving a thirty-foot motorhome on Mexico's narrow, and sometimes potholed or unpaved, streets was enough of a challenge.

Once we left Tijuana, most of the traffic disappeared. After driving south for about an hour, it was time to stop for Karen's lobster dinner. We parked the motorhomes in a gravel lot a few blocks away from the restaurant. I had to leave Rylie in the Green Monster while we ate, and I felt uneasiness creep over me. Signs of poverty were everywhere, and my new $85,000 motorhome seemed conspicuous. After reading all of the stories of crime in Mexico, I didn't know if it was safe to leave Rylie or the motorhome unattended in this town. *Will they be here when I get back?* I cast nervous glances over my shoulder as I walked away from the motorhome.

Throughout our meal I kept checking my watch, anxious to get Rylie and the Green Monster back in sight. I couldn't relax and enjoy myself and barely tasted my food. I controlled my urge to speed-walk after dinner as we made our way back to the parking lot. When those distinctive green and white stripes came into view with Rylie sitting patiently in the passenger seat, I emptied my lungs in a whoosh of relief, then laughed at my silly fears. *No one is going to break into the motorhome with Rylie keeping watch in the front seat. Relax, Heidi.*

We drove about another hour before stopping for the night as the sun was slinking toward the horizon. We parked in a dark, deserted lot perched on a bluff above the restless Pacific Ocean and gathered in our camp chairs to toast our first night in Mexico.

"Here's to the Baja Babes," Lucy declared as we clinked our plastic wineglasses.

"To the Baja Babes," we echoed, laughing.

I took a deep breath, the ocean mix of salt, seaweed, and fish filling my nostrils. I felt my muscles and nerves unclenching from the stress of navigating the Green Monster through the unfamiliar, narrow roads and traffic. I sipped my wine and looked around at my traveling companions. Karen was in her sixties and tall, with rosy cheeks and a helmet of dark curls. Elaine was a bit younger and shorter, with wispy blond hair and a stocky build. All three women had a good sense of humor, but Lucy was especially funny. She had a passionate nature, and she did everything with great gusto, whether she was giggling at a funny story she'd just told or chewing out someone who was rude. We were all animal lovers. Our little caravan contained four dogs and one cat.

After we said good night and tucked into our respective motorhomes, the scary stories I'd heard about crime in Mexico popped into my head again. I felt like we were four sitting ducks in our brightly painted motorhomes in a deserted lot just off the highway. The waves of the Pacific seemed to be rumbling a warning. I soothed myself with the thought that there was strength in numbers. Glad that I had Rylie for company, I kept him close as I drifted into a troubled sleep. Although this night passed peacefully, I wasn't so lucky the next night.

CHAPTER 9

NIGHT TERROR

FEBRUARY 2007

I'll tell you what freedom is to me: no fear.

—Nina Simone

The next day we slowly made our way south, passing through small towns wearing the tattered stamps of poverty. We often saw simple half-built homes standing in their cement-and-rebar skeletons, waiting for an infusion of cash to finish them. Despite the poor economy in these towns, they were always splashed with bright colors, which lent an air of hopefulness and festivity. In the afternoon we stopped for the day next to an enormous stretch of barren beach on the Pacific Ocean. Although this was labeled a campground in our Baja travel book, it wasn't what we would call a campground in the States. There were no hookups, fire pits, or picnic tables; it was simply a sandy, secluded spot off a side road where we could park the motorhomes. There was a sign indicating the manager lived down at the far end of the road, although we never saw him until the following morning. As far as I could tell, we were the only ones camped there.

After settling in, I took Rylie out for a walk on the beach and let him off the leash, since dogs are rarely leashed in Baja.

I smiled while watching him race around in the sand, stopping now and then for some furious digging. He steered clear of the water, but his joyful shoveling told me he loved the beach. I could tell he was feeling his newly found freedom just as keenly as I was feeling mine. I had no work schedule holding us captive and no major home or yard chores. Best of all, our senses were flooded every day with new sights, new smells, and new friends. My heart felt as if it could float into the air like dandelion fluff on a summer day.

The four motorhomes in our caravan huddled close together in a secluded alcove of bushes next to the beach. As evening approached, we once again gathered in our camp chairs for appetizers and a glass of wine. Soon a dog wandered into our campsite, begging for food. This set off a round of barking among Elaine's three German shepherds and Rylie, creating quite a racket.

Once the dogs were all properly introduced from a distance and they saw there was no threat from this life-worn hound, they all settled down. Our visitor was a medium-sized mutt, and her spotted fur was matted and missing in patches. The haunted look in her eyes told us her life had not been easy. Elaine took pity and donated some of her dog kibble and water to our straggly visitor.

The number of stray animals in Baja was heartbreaking. Mexico didn't have the number of rescue organizations for animals that we had in the States, and it was a much harder life for dogs there. Many of them wandered the streets scrounging up food in trash bags, outside the back doors of restaurants, or anywhere else they could find it. Even when a dog "belonged" to someone, they still wandered around loose and begged for food. Often, they hadn't been spayed or neutered, so they mated in the streets. This resulted in an overpopulation problem, with little money or resources to deal with these unwanted pooches. Getting the basic medical care they needed, like vaccinations and deworming, was the exception rather than the norm. I wanted to save all of the dogs I saw and bring them back to the States with me, and my caravan companions felt the same way. We were a bunch of softies where animals were concerned.

Our new friend stuck close by after finishing her meal, hoping for a second course, which Elaine was happy to provide. A bit later a young puppy appeared, clearly waiting nearby for his mom. I fetched some of Rylie's smaller-sized kibble and put it into a paper bowl. The puppy wolfed down the kibble, and both he and his mom had a drink of water. The puppy was a fluffy ball of ginger-brown fur, so it was hard to tell how thin he was, but he had rheumy eyes and didn't look well.

"Poor little guy," I said. "Life is tough for you already, isn't it? And you've barely started." Both mom and pup hunkered down in our camp as evening pulled the shade of darkness closer. Eventually, the yawning took over our group and we doused the fire.

"I don't think we dare let these dogs into our motorhomes," Elaine said. "There's no telling what diseases they might have, and parvo could be deadly for our dogs. After seeing all of the scratching they're doing, I think they must have fleas, at the very least."

I agreed and reluctantly bade mom and pup good night as we all turned in for the night, tired from our day of driving. We assumed they would go back to wherever they'd come from. I drifted off to sleep with Rylie on the bed near my feet, as usual.

Halfway through the night, Rylie leaped off the bed and tore to the front of the motorhome, barking wildly. I awoke terrified, not knowing what caused this ferocious warning. Rylie almost never barked in the middle of the night, and he never barked this frantically. I could hear Elaine's dogs making an even louder racket in her motorhome. *Someone is out there.* I tried to shake off the cobwebs of sleep and listen for the sound of intruders but couldn't hear anything over the racket from the dogs.

The driver's and front passenger seats of my motorhome were separated from the living area by a short curtain that I closed during the night. I could duck under it to access the seats, and Rylie could walk freely on the floor beneath it. He jumped into the passenger seat of the motorhome, where he could look outside, still barking furiously. I peeked beneath the curtain but couldn't see anything in the blackness. I turned on my headlights but still saw nothing other than the motorhomes and the dark, shadowy shapes of sand dunes and bushes beyond them.

I didn't dare go outside, because I didn't know what was out there. *Is it the evil banditos I've heard so many stories about, coming to rob the motorhomes—or worse?* The staccato pounding of my heart jumping against my ribs and the adrenaline burning through my veins transformed my breathing to shallow panting. I had no weapons with which to protect myself, except the kitchen knives. I could almost smell my fear as I grabbed the largest knife out of the butcher's block, wondering if I would have the guts to use it if I had to.

While my mind scrambled to decide what to do, I heard the unmistakable yelping and whining of coyotes. First, they were close, then the sound moved away from the motorhomes. I realized they must have been after the puppy, and maybe his mother, but the loud barking from the German shepherds and Rylie had scared them off. At least I hoped so. I was too frightened to go outside and check. My jumping heart eventually began to still as I realized it was only coyotes circling the motorhomes and not the more dangerous possibility—humans.

It took some time for the adrenaline to fully drain from my system and I slept fitfully the rest of the night. I worried about what I might discover in the morning. Once the sun was up,

I stepped outside. The sound of the door and my feet on the steps brought the mother and pup out from under my motorhome, looking for breakfast. They were using my vehicle as their shelter from the coyotes. All of my fears turned out to be a figment of my active imagination, fueled by the crime stories I'd read before entering Baja.

I was so relieved and grateful that our furry companions had kept the coyotes at bay with their fierce warnings, I almost cried. The barking dogs saved at least one life—the puppy's—and maybe the mother's, too. I gave Rylie an extra treat with his breakfast, and the mother and pup, too.

Before we left the campground, Lucy stopped to talk to the campground manager and later relayed the conversation.

"Do you know who these dogs belong to?" Lucy asked the manager.

"*Sí*, they live here," the manager replied.

"Well you better keep them in at night," Lucy said. "They were almost dinner for the coyotes last night."

"*Sí, señora*, I take care of them," the manager assured her.

There was nothing more we could do, so we continued on our way, hoping our new furry friends would be safe.

CHAPTER 10

THE HUSBAND CONUNDRUM

FEBRUARY 2007

*. . . then I wonder, does anyone ever intend on being that
kind of person?*

—Stevie J. Cole

T he first time the soldiers entered my motorhome, I did my
best to hide my alarm. *Stay calm. You have no reason to be
nervous.* I was stopped at the first of many military checkpoints
I encountered in Baja. Each time, young, uniformed soldiers
with semiautomatic weapons milled around the checkpoint and
then entered my motorhome to conduct a search. It wasn't
entirely clear to me what they were looking for. At this initial
stop, the first soldier at the door took one look at Rylie and,
before entering, asked in Spanish, "*¿Muerde el perro?*" Since my
Spanish was extremely limited, I had no idea what he was
asking me.

Seeing the confused look on my face, one of the other
soldiers asked in English, "Does the dog bite?"

"No, he won't bite," I assured them.

"Where is your husband?" asked another soldier in heavily
accented English as he looked suspiciously around the interior
of my motorhome.

"I don't have a husband." The soldiers looked disappointed.

Three soldiers then entered, and while I sat on the sofa with Rylie at my side, they searched my motorhome. They looked in the bedroom, the closets, the bathroom, and the shower. *Are they looking for stowaways? Drugs? Weapons? What kind of mischief do they think I'm up to?* Then they moved on to the refrigerator, the pantry, and the cupboards. With three of them searching, it took no more than five minutes, then they sent me on my way.

At the next checkpoint, the process was repeated. They asked if the dog bit, asked where my husband was, and then conducted their search. After several repeats of this I got used to the routine and began to think of it as an inconvenient delay more than anything to be concerned about.

The next time I was asked where my husband was, I sighed inwardly and contemplated my response. This question was asked of not only me, but also my caravan of single ladies, each time we entered a checkpoint. Clearly, the soldiers disapproved of women traveling without husbands. Someone told us later that Mexican women did not travel without husbands very much. Finding four of us all at once, each in her own motorhome—unescorted and on the loose—didn't seem to sit right with them.

"In the refrigerator," I was tempted to reply. My fridge was about half the size of a normal refrigerator and could only accommodate a husband if he were in pieces.

"Hiding in the shower with the drugs," was another option, but somehow, I didn't think these solemn-faced soldiers would find that funny.

I decided to play it straight and told the soldier, "*No esposo.*" No husband. I was gaining Spanish, bit by bit.

The soldier opened a few drawers, the bathroom and shower doors, and the refrigerator. Then, seeing the refrigerator contents, asked for a Coke.

"I only have Diet Coke," I replied. "Would you like one?"

He did want one. He asked if he could have three more for his friends. I thought that was a bit strange, but I handed them over with a smile. He thanked me for the Diet Cokes and sent me on my way. It wasn't until I was at the next military checkpoint that I realized the soldiers were selling cans of soda for a buck apiece.

At the next checkpoint, there it was again. "Where is your husband?" Three soldiers this time.

I shrugged my shoulders and lifted my arms, palms up, as if to say, "Who knows?" I sat on the sofa with Rylie at my side while they searched the bedroom. It seemed to be taking longer than usual, so eventually I went to the bedroom to see what was causing the delay. I saw the three of them huddled on the right side of the bed whispering among themselves in Spanish, next to an open drawer. My lingerie drawer. As soon as they saw me, they stopped talking and started moving toward the door. *Did the drawer open while I was driving, or did they open it? What were they talking about?* I never found out. They left the motorhome and I was waved through the checkpoint.

At another checkpoint, I was asked yet again where my husband was.

"No husband," was my weary response.

"No husband?" asked the baby-faced soldier, who was barely pushing twenty years old. He looked around my shiny new motorhome with its queen-sized bed, flat-screen TV, and comfy sofa, and smiled. "Can I have your phone number? I love you."

"No, you can't have my phone number!" I scolded. "I'm old enough to be your mother!"

Throughout my travels it seemed that either there weren't enough husbands, or else there were too many—too many of other women's husbands. I met many people during my travels. I met women traveling alone, and these women were almost always single. I also met couples, and we would sometimes socialize together. Rarely, I ran into single men traveling alone. Then there were the men who were traveling for work. They were almost always married, but some of them tried very hard to hide that little detail.

"We're kind of separated right now," one longtime married man said when I asked about his wife. The truth was that he was in Texas, and his wife was in Canada. They were geographically separated by his work, not legally separated.

"We're not together," said another of his wife. It turned out that his wife was out shopping. Technically, they weren't lying, but they were certainly trying to give the wrong impression.

It seemed that everywhere I went I ran into married men who were trying to see what they could get away with. For some reason, they thought I was a good candidate for their shenanigans. It finally dawned on me why I was running into so many overly friendly married men. I was traveling around the country in a motorhome, which meant that I would not be staying in any one place for very long. These married men didn't have to worry about any messy entanglements, because they knew that I was a single traveler, and before long, I would be moving on. I was the perfect victim for a drive-by fling.

The next time I met a married man on the prowl, I was ready.

"My wife and I are separated," he said, with his wife's sunglasses sitting on the picnic table.

"Perfect!" I said with a wicked smile. "My husband is in the refrigerator."

CHAPTER 11

LIFE ON THE BEACH

FEBRUARY 2007

To escape and sit quietly on the beach—that's my idea of paradise.

—Emilia Wickstead

"El Coyote, here we come!" Lucy was on the CB radio, letting us know that we were nearing our destination, El Coyote Beach. While we were traveling, she'd exchanged emails with Frankie and Stan, a couple she knew who spent every winter on the beach. In my Baja travel book, I'd learned this postcard-pretty beach hugged an emerald bay on the Sea of Cortez south of Mulegé. We planned to spend some time with Frankie and Stan on the beach before heading to Magdalena Bay on the Pacific Ocean to see the gray whales and their newborn calves.

When we reached the entrance to El Coyote Beach, Lucy called Frankie and Stan to let them know we'd arrived. Stan hurried over in their Jeep, parked, and hopped out to help us through the tricky entrance. He was a sturdy man in his early sixties in shorts and a T-shirt who wore a cap down to his ears, so his hair was an unsolved mystery. I could tell by his easy grin that he was a good-natured guy.

"This entrance can be a bit tricky," he told us through our open windows. "I'll guide you."

Once I saw the road, I was happy for his help. The skinny dirt road on the north end of the bay squeezed between the rocky wall of the hillside on the right and the sea on the left, with jagged-tooth boulders poking up all over the place. Stan waved each of us this way and that to skirt the rocks and keep us from plunging into the water on the other side. I squeezed through the obstacle course unscathed, but Lucy wasn't as lucky. One of the boulders bit the side of her motorhome as she struggled to follow Stan's hand signals, leaving a small scrape. In her customary carefree style, Lucy waved away our concern.

"It's not the first scrape I've gotten, and it won't be the last. Don't worry about it—I'm not."

The tricky entrance was well worth the trouble. We parked right next to the beach with a gorgeous front-row view of the bay. Motorhomes and trailers lined the sand, and a sailboat was serenely anchored on the south side of the bay. Surrounding the bay were desert-scrub-studded hillsides, with the Baja Highway perched far above us. I parked my motorhome and walked outside with Rylie to meet the neighbors, my nostrils filling with the familiar smell of the sea, punctuated by the occasional squawk of gulls flying overhead.

After proper introductions with Stan, we met his wife, Frankie. Frankie was in her fifties, with the well-muscled calves of a hiker and a fluff of gray hair. We learned they'd retired early and left their house in the US every winter to spend several months on El Coyote Beach. They introduced us to Will and Brenda, retired teachers who said they'd spent the past couple of weeks on the beach but were heading back to the States in a week. Next was Ray, a tanned, silver-bearded guy in his mid-seventies. It soon became obvious he still considered himself the Casanova from his youth, strutting around in his Speedo and flirting with the single ladies.

As we settled in our camp chairs on the beach, I learned that Frankie and Stan were friendly, active, and funny. They loved hiking, kayaking, exploring, and adventure, and were always willing to lend a helping hand to anyone who needed it.

One day, I stepped outside of my motorhome and discovered one of the tires was flat. *Uh-oh, the Green Monster is up to some mischief. That's okay, I can handle this.* I'd prepared for this possibility by buying an air compressor before starting my travels. I had never bought a compressor before, but I checked to make sure the pressure limits listed on the box went beyond the pressure of my motorhome tires. It seemed pretty straightforward. Although I hadn't used it yet, I felt confident. *I'll show everyone how prepared I am, and that I'm not some damsel in distress.*

I fetched the air compressor from the storage bin, turned on the motorhome generator for electricity, plugged in the compressor, and started putting air in the tire. After a few minutes, the tire looked the same. I ran the compressor longer, then checked the pressure on my gauge, but the tire had barely inflated. The instructions warned not to run the compressor too long or it would overheat, so I kept shutting it off to let it cool down. A half hour later, the tire still was not inflated. My frustration grew and my confidence sagged. *I guess I'm a damsel in distress after all. Where did I go wrong, and what do I do now?* I felt fear seeping in, overpowering my frustration.

Stan saw me struggling and took pity on me. "I have a bottle of compressed air, and it will fill your tire in about thirty seconds. Would you like me to bring it over?"

"I sure would," I said, grateful for his help. He filled my tire and then he, Frankie, and Lucy followed me with their car during the drive into Mulegé to make sure I made it to a tire repair shop without any problems. The tire was patched and I was soon on my way. Later I was told I needed a more powerful air compressor, despite what was printed on the box. Mine was useless for the motorhome, just an $80 lesson learned.

Stan came to the rescue of many people—especially the women traveling alone—when something mechanical broke on their motorhomes. At one point, the CB antenna on top of my motorhome got knocked out of commission, and Stan offered to climb up onto my roof and fix it. Stan and Frankie both had hearts of gold and were such fun to be around. Frankie always invited us to join in whatever fun they had planned for the day, and it was easy to fall into friendship with this openhearted couple.

We immediately became part of Frankie and Stan's community, which consisted of an interesting assortment of RV dwellers of all ages. Most were American and Canadian, but there was a young British/German couple, Ellie and Franz, as well as a few others from various countries. Some came and went in a matter of days or weeks, and others stayed for months. The regulars, like Frankie and Stan, came every winter.

It was a well-organized group, expanding and contracting with the continual arrival and departure of the people who didn't stay for the season. There were many social activities, including coffee on the beach in the morning, cocktail hour with appetizers and campfires every evening, and occasional potluck dinners. Each day was filled with something fun or interesting. Sometimes we crammed into the available cars and went to town or explored the area. Other times we piled into the inflatable boats to go snorkeling, clamming, or over to Bertha's restaurant for lunch and an icy cold cerveza. We went hiking and kayaking, rode quads, played games, watched movies, and read books.

Everyone shared what they had, from kayaks to inflatable water toys to food, and hours were spent paddling or floating in the bay. Palapas, which are very basic huts made from palm fronds and bamboo, dotted the beach. These were used to store toys and extra gear or put to other creative uses. One was made into an extended kitchen, and another was converted to an internet café. We could sit in the shade of the palapa and, using the satellite internet connection from one of the motorhomes, check our email or search the web. The palapa near Frankie and Stan's motorhome contained the library, where we could trade books and movies. There was always something to do or someone to talk with if you felt like it, or you could disappear for some quiet time alone in your RV.

There were no electrical or other hookups on the beach, so those of us who had solar panels on our RVs relied on the sun for electricity. We got used to going to bed early, because once darkness fell, the lights or TV would start running down the batteries. It was considered rude to run generators because they disturbed the serenity of beach living, so they were run rarely, and only when absolutely necessary.

Just about everything we needed was sold to us on the beach by the locals, including water for our fresh-water tanks, fuel for our propane tanks to run the refrigerators and water heaters, fresh seafood, and even fruits and vegetables. One woman brought delicious homemade empanadas every morning filled with pineapple or other fruit. The only thing missing was a place to empty our sewage and wastewater tanks, but we could drive to a dumping station at a nearby beach for that. The locals also brought their colorful handicrafts to peddle, including pottery, jewelry, clothing, woven blankets, and other trinkets. It was an idyllic life, and I reveled in it.

One day, we gathered a group and took two Zodiacs out to explore the nearby shoreline. We stopped at another beach and waded in to see if we could find some clams. As I wandered in the shin-deep coolness, I turned to look behind me and saw a small ray swimming right behind me, its body undulating like wings. I saw two more rays following it. They seemed curious about what we were up to. I was delighted—I had never seen a ray before. They quickly swam away when they were discovered.

After gathering some clams, we got back into the boats and started motoring over to Bertha's café for lunch. As the Zodiacs sped through the water, a pod of fun-seeking dolphins suddenly appeared. A few of them stuck right next to the bows of both boats, as though they were escorting us. Their sleek heads zipped in and out of the water as they sped along at top speed. They were close enough to touch if we leaned over.

"They're so fast!" I said, laughing out loud at their playful antics. Eventually, they swam off for a new amusement. This life on the beach was pure joy for me, and I couldn't believe my good fortune. I could spend hours playing in the water, reading, or relaxing with friends. I didn't have to worry about returning to work, paying bills, or taking care of anyone other than myself and Rylie. This was the total freedom I had longed for, and I relished it with joyful abandon. Not only did I have the luxury of time and freedom, but I'd found a community. I no longer felt like an outsider—that I didn't fit in. *I belong here.*

CHAPTER 12

THE GIFT

FEBRUARY 2007

The sea, once it casts its spell, holds one in its net of
wonder forever.

—Jacques-Yves Cousteau

I stood barefoot and alone in the cool sand of El Coyote Beach, surrounded by the cloak of the black-velvet night. It was the kind of darkness that can only be experienced when you escape from the bustle and bright lights of civilization. Looking up, I searched for the constellations that were usually so brilliant and plentiful above the Sea of Cortez, but the clouds had been stitching themselves together throughout the day, creating a puffy layer of insulation that hid the twinkling trails of stars.

I wandered down the beach toward the usual spot for the evening campfire and came upon Frankie standing near the water.

"Heidi, did you see the water?" Frankie asked.

I turned to look at the sea and saw several other people splashing and kayaking in the shallow water. Whenever the water was disturbed with a splash, boat, or paddle, it would glitter as though buckets of diamonds had been scattered into the sea.

"It's so beautiful!" I kicked off my flip-flops and ran into the water. "What is it?"

"Bioluminescence. Have you ever seen it before?" Frankie asked. "It's from tiny sea organisms."

"Never. I've heard of it, but I had no idea it was this amazing. So that must be what I saw in the water earlier today." I'd spent hours that day frolicking in the warm bay like a kid during summer vacation, swimming and lazily floating around on my inflatable tube. When I neared the shore, I saw a frothy foam where the sea met the sand. Now I knew this was from tiny organisms that produced the bioluminescence. These little, light-filled creatures put on an amazing show.

We splashed along the shore and paddled in kayaks for a long time, delighting in the water shimmering with every stroke. When we were done in the water, we gathered around the campfire, happiness spilling throughout our conversation as we experienced this special show from Mother Nature. Eventually, the last licks of the campfire turned to ash, and everyone murmured their good nights as they wandered off to bed. Reluctant to let go of this unusual experience, I was the last one lingering on the beach.

As I trudged slowly through the sand back to my motorhome, my dawdling brought me a precious gift. A light rain began spattering through the warm air, and as the drops hit the water, it winked and flashed in the darkness. The entire sea looked like it was filled with glittering fairy dust, and it was the most magical sight I have ever seen. I caught my breath and, for a moment, felt as though the world had flipped upside down and billions of stars were now bathing in the bay.

My heart was flooded with happiness, and I was reminded of what I felt when my daughter was born. After the pain of labor, an overwhelming sense of wonder at the miracle of life and my part in it had me drenched in euphoria. This time I was a mere spectator to this fantasia of nature, but it was still a transformative moment for me.

For years, I had been closed off to joy and the beauty of nature and life surrounding me. The pain from years of struggle and emotional suffering had me so thoroughly wrapped up in my cape of unhappiness; I lost my passion for living and the wonder of nature. My loneliness and despair once had me teetering on the brink with suicidal thoughts before I realized I had other options for escape.

I knew I'd made the right decision when I decided to embark on this journey. Leaving the conventional life of the "American dream" behind to take a solo journey to recover my spirit was a life-changing decision. I had crawled through the dark tunnel and made it to the brilliant sunshine at the other end. My eyes were opened.

Witnessing Mother Nature's incredible water show was somehow so personal, and because I was by myself, it seemed intended just for me. I was a solo traveler on an empty beach witnessing a magical moment. Although I had no special someone to share it with, I didn't feel the least bit lonely. This performance seemed like it was choreographed for an audience of one, as though a gorgeous and talented dancing partner were holding out a hand and inviting me to rejoin the dance.

I quick-stepped into the sea again, smiling as the blinking water shimmered around my ankles and warm raindrops tickled my skin. I felt certain I was meant to be here, in this moment, and I realized how completely my life had turned around. I felt connected to the universe, like I was a tiny but integral part of it. I'd learned that even when life looks very bleak and we are certain the future holds nothing but hard work, loneliness, and sorrow, good things can be waiting right around the corner. My world *had* turned upside down, and it was for the better.

This experience opened me up to a sense of awe and wonder about the world that I hadn't felt since I was a child. Emotion washed over me, but instead of tears, laughter welled up inside and spilled out my throat. I knew how special it was to be in this moment, full of life and love, and grateful to be alive. It made all of the struggles and strife of my lonely childhood, draining divorce, single parenthood, and sagging confidence in myself melt away, and in their place was a new-found happiness, and a deep-in-the-soul knowledge that everything was okay—I was okay. The knowledge that I had been ready to give up when this wonderful adventure was just around the corner made me giddy with gratitude.

Later, when I told other women about my solo travels in a motorhome, some would tell me how brave I was. At the time, I didn't think of my decision as brave. I thought it was necessary for my sanity and survival. Running away in middle age saved my life.

CHAPTER 13

ANOTHER DEAD BODY

FEBRUARY 2007

Fortune favors the bold.

—Latin proverb

With the discovery of the old man, that made a total of two dead bodies found in my neighborhood. That is, if an RV traveler can have a neighborhood. The dead hiker in New Mexico had been troubling, but the old man's death brought tears to my eyes and left me aching with sadness. That might seem strange, because I didn't even know him. The old man was a weathered fisherman chasing ninety years of age, who lived just up the beach in a six-by-six tent with his equally weathered, but younger, brother.

Twice every day, Rylie and I walked the entire length of the bay, which brought us right past the place where the brothers lived. The older brother never acknowledged us, but the younger brother would smile and greet me, though with my sparse Spanish and his limited English, we could never exchange more than a few words. He seemed happy and friendly but appeared very poor. I started to look forward to our exchanges, as brief as they were, because he always seemed so appreciative of each and every day.

"What's the story with the old fishermen at the other end of the beach?" I asked Frankie one day.

"I heard those two have lived there in that tent for years. I guess they're homeless by choice."

"They seem happy. I guess they have everything they want." The next time I walked by, I looked more closely at their camp. A sturdy wooden fishing panga was casually tied to a tree. Their tent, pitched in the shade, provided minimal shelter against the chilly winter winds, but this breathtaking bay on the Sea of Cortez provided the most beautiful front yard anyone could want. A few cooking pots were littered around their fire pit, along with various other signs of long-term residency.

It was not far from this campsite where they found the older brother's body. A police car looked out of place parked near the beach, and as I walked past, I could see two policemen talking to the people camped nearby.

One evening shortly after I arrived on the beach, we were discussing the dangers we'd heard about. Someone mentioned that another camper's kayak had been stolen from the palapa next to their motorhome.

"Let's form a neighborhood watch," one member of the group suggested. "If you hear or see something suspicious, honk your horn." Several of the others agreed.

"Okay," I said. "I will, too."

At around midnight that very same evening, I awoke to the sound of hushed voices. They were coming from the palapa next to my motorhome, which contained the kayaks and other gear of my neighbors. I remembered the conversation earlier about someone having their kayak stolen. I was so ready for trouble, I immediately assumed my neighbors were about to be robbed. I peeked out the window to see if I could tell who was out there. Whoever it was, they were not using flashlights. *They must be intruders!*

I hurried to the cab of my motorhome and honked the horn, turned on my CB radio, and asked if anyone could hear me. Karen, who was parked down the beach a few motorhomes away, was the only one awake and listening, but she wasn't interested in investigating. After sneaking a peek outside, I discovered that a couple of local lovers seeking some privacy had chosen the palapa to be their little love shack. The loud honking apparently spoiled the mood, and they were walking away, adjusting their clothing.

I sheepishly returned to bed, fully realizing the power of suggestion. Even though nothing in my experience while traveling in Baja had demonstrated danger, crime, or corruption, I'd bought into the fears that Mexico was a scary place full of hooligans and scalawags. I was embarrassed.

I was the butt of many jokes among my beach companions during the next few days, but I learned an important lesson. The people of Baja weren't out to get us; they were just trying to make a living and find a little bit of happiness. That's what most of us want.

It turned out the discovery of the old man's body was not a cause for suspicion. He'd died of a heart attack while fishing. The next time I walked Rylie down to the end of the beach where the brothers camped, my heart sank. Where the tent had been, a few discarded possessions were all that remained of the home they'd loved. It made me feel incredibly sad for the younger brother, that he had to give up his lovely spot on the beach. I wondered if it was his decision to leave, or whether someone else had decided that an old man shouldn't live on the beach by himself. I hope he didn't end up in a nursing home with beige walls, bad smells, and fluorescent lights. It probably would have killed him.

Chapter 14

Meeting Whales

February 2007

My soul is full of longing for the secret of the sea.

—Henry Wadsworth Longfellow

I clutched the wooden bench tightly as the fishing panga thumped through the waves of Magdalena Bay on the Pacific Ocean, my body a live wire of excited anticipation. I'd eagerly looked forward to this day ever since crossing the border into the Baja Peninsula two weeks earlier. I'd known when I started planning this Mexican excursion that this experience would be one of the highlights of the trip. *I'm meeting the whales!*

Every year the gray whales migrated ten thousand miles from their summer feeding grounds in Alaska to the warmer waters of Mexico. During the months of January through April they mated, gave birth, and fed their young. February was the best month to see newborn calves in three areas along the coast: San Ignacio Lagoon, Scammon's Lagoon, and Magdalena Bay. The latter was the furthest south, and it was only 150 miles from my campsite on El Coyote Beach.

My small caravan for the whale-watching trip included the same three companions who had crossed the border with me:

Lucy, Karen, and Elaine. When we arrived at Magdalena Bay we bought tickets for a boat the next day at a small shack near the water and camped for the night in the dirt lot next to it. Early the next morning, we went to the designated departure spot.

We were loaded onto a small wooden fishing boat along with our captain, a well-fed middle-aged man with fair English who was also our guide. There might have been enough room to squeeze a couple more people into the small boat, but that was it. It was vastly different from the whale-watching boats I had been on before. Those boats were behemoths compared to this little panga, and sometimes held dozens of people. In the US, whale-watching vessels were not allowed to get closer than one hundred yards from whales, to prevent whales from being harassed by overly eager whale watchers. Mexico did not have the same regulations, so we were allowed to get closer.

During my previous whale-watching trips in California and Hawaii we'd managed to find a few whales, but they were always viewed from a distance. I had serious reservations about coming too close to the whales and potentially causing them stress. I soon learned that there was no cause for concern. This was a very different experience, and definitely friendly. As we motored to the area where the captain said we would find mothers with newborn calves, we passed the bay's opening to the Pacific.

"Look, whales!" Lucy exclaimed, pointing excitedly off in the distance. We could see whales cavorting through the bigger waves of the Pacific.

"Those are the males," our captain explained. "They are putting on a show so they can get the females."

The whales breached the surface over and over again, their heavy bodies slamming into the water. Even from far away, we could hear the loud smacks. Some whales were spy-hopping, sticking their enormous heads straight up out of the water and back down again, as though they were hopping on their tails.

"We're going to stay in the bay where the mothers and babies are," the captain said. "The water is calmer there." We continued on, and it wasn't long until we started seeing whales very close by. A few other whale-watching boats were also in the area, and occasionally the boats would gather near the same whales. But there were at least a dozen whales nearby, plenty to give each boat an up-close-and-personal experience.

"Over there, look!" Lucy called out excitedly, pointing at a nearby whale.

"That mama has a newborn," the captain said. He steered the boat in the whale's direction, and we all scrambled for our cameras. The boat, which had seemed pretty small when we left the dock, felt downright tiny once we got next to some whales. Adult gray whales are approximately fifty feet long and weigh thirty-six tons. I realized that our sixteen-foot panga could be flipped like a tiddlywink by these huge creatures three times that size.

"You see the knuckles on the baby's spine?" the captain asked. Bumps along the calf's spine looked like the knuckles on human hands. "Those go away in a few days when the baby starts gaining weight."

I expected the mother whale to swim away as we got closer, but she didn't. In fact, she didn't seem to mind our presence at all and willingly stayed with us for a long time. My reservations about getting too close to the whales disappeared when I realized that these whales seemed just as curious about us as we were about them. Mother and calf kept swimming back and forth next to and right beneath our boat. I had never been so close to whales, and especially to a newborn. At one point, they came right next to the boat and the mother looked at us with one eye out of the water. She gazed at us leisurely, as though she was studying us. I longed to know what she was thinking.

Flowerlike barnacles had attached themselves to the back and sides of the mother, but the calf was too young to have sprouted that garden. Both whales came close enough to our boat to reach out and touch, and then swam over to one of the other boats. We watched as a woman in the other boat touched the fin the newborn raised against their boat.

"Wow!" Lucy exclaimed. "It looks like that baby wants to shake hands."

Both mother and baby seemed unafraid of the gawking humans gathered around, excitedly snapping photos. Maybe she wanted her calf to meet humans, or they were just curious—I will never know. But every now and then I think about this whale encounter, and I wonder why this mother and calf hung out with us for so long.

Neither the mother nor the baby even grazed the boats, except for the newborn's one-fin handshake. I was amazed at how they could get so close but never bump us. A simple flick of the mother's tail could have capsized the boat, but she was careful. She seemed to be enjoying us almost as much as we were enjoying her.

Emotion tightened my throat, and I struggled to identify what I was feeling. Gratitude. I was so grateful for this intimate encounter. These gentle, friendly whales made me want to know more about them. There was something else, though. It was longing. I wished that we could communicate somehow. *What do they think of us?*

I thought of all of the terrible things that humans have done to so many species. Not only did people hunt whales, but baby whales were stolen and raised in small tanks for entertainment, where they slowly lost their minds from stress and boredom. We also polluted and destroyed their habitat. I felt suddenly protective of our new friends. I wanted to let them know that not all humans wished to do them harm. There was no way to communicate that, but maybe these whales already knew it.

CHAPTER 15

BLUE EYES

MARCH 2007

Words are, of course, the most powerful drug used
by mankind.

—Rudyard Kipling

All too soon a month had flown by, and it was time for Karen and Elaine to return to the US. I reluctantly hugged them goodbye, with promises to stay in touch. Lucy and I decided to explore the lower half of the Baja Peninsula together. We stopped for a few days in La Paz, where we could camp for free on the beach.

La Paz, the capital of the state of Baja California Sur, sat on a bay on the Sea of Cortez and had a population of about two hundred thousand people. The Malecón ran along the coast, rimmed by a generous sidewalk to accommodate the crowds of people visiting the many colorful restaurants and festive cantinas on foot. We were headed for an enormous public beach with wide swaths of sand that was rumored to be a jackpot for shell seekers.

I trailed Lucy's motorhome as we entered the camping area but hung back with an uneasy feeling when I saw her heading into an area with drifts of loose sand. It looked like trouble, and it was. The rear wheels of Lucy's motorhome got stuck in the sand and spun when she hit the gas. Rocking the motorhome from drive to reverse didn't free them.

It was early March and the wind was blasting. The wind-whipped sand stung our faces when we left the motorhomes to work on freeing the wheels. Lucy had a two-by-four that she tried to use for traction under the wheels on one side, but still they sputtered and refused to budge. I got out my leveling blocks, thinking we could make a path with those, but they just got buried in the sand. We tried digging out the sand with small containers that Lucy provided, but more sand slid in to fill its place.

Finally, a man emerged from a motorhome up the beach and walked toward us, leaning into the wind as he approached. He was tall and lean, with a head full of gray hair and a jacket zipped up to his chin.

"Hi, I'm Jim. Would you like some help?" We gratefully accepted. Jim went to retrieve a shovel from his motorhome and quickly shoveled enough sand to get the leveling blocks under the wheels. Lucy backed onto them and out of the sand, but not before breaking one of them.

"Don't worry about it," I assured Lucy, who was distraught at having destroyed one of my leveling blocks. "I have plenty more." We thanked Jim profusely, gave him a bottle of wine, and drove off to find a safer place to park the motorhomes.

After the wind died down we wandered over to a shack near the dock in search of a snorkel trip. We wanted to visit a beautiful island just offshore called Isla Espíritu Santo. This uninhabited island was known as an ecotourism destination. A brochure for an excursion to the island showed a white-sand beach flanked by turquoise water, ideal for snorkeling. The trip included a picnic lunch. We reserved two seats on a boat for the following day.

As we boarded the wooden boat the next day, I couldn't keep my eyes off the captain. He had some of the bluest eyes I had ever seen on a man, and they looked even bluer in his handsome, tanned face. Captain Juan's wavy black hair was the kind you want to run your fingers through, and his dazzling smile was enough to charm more than his fair share of the ladies. He appeared to be in his forties with his bright azure eyes, which were very unusual in these parts. The female species didn't stand a chance.

He handled the boat with ease, as though it were another limb of his body, rather than a twenty-foot vessel packed to the brim with passengers. He moved nimbly from the bow of the boat to the stern, stepping lightly on the benches between passengers like a smooth stone skipping on water. When he stepped next to me, his fingers grazed my shoulder lightly as though for balance, but his natural sure-footedness belied the need for my shoulder. I felt a flutter inside at his touch and my pulse quickened.

He spoke only in his native tongue, and my limited Spanish caught only occasional words, but the first mate spoke English for the mostly gringo passengers. The captain pointed out the interesting rock formations, seabirds, and other sights, and the first mate spoon-fed us bits of history and humor along the way. The plan was to stop and swim with the sea lions for those who wanted an animal encounter, then head to the beautiful bay of Espíritu Santo for snorkeling.

On the way to the island, Captain Juan stopped the boat so we could photograph or swim with the sea lions. The water was deeper and colder here and it was still early in the season, so only a few brave souls got in the water to swim, while the rest of us stayed in the boat to take photographs. The captain, wearing a short wetsuit, dove into the water and resurfaced next to me a few moments later with a starfish in his hand and another dazzling smile. He was even more handsome when he was soaking wet, if that was possible. I smiled back. I'll admit that I was more interested in the handsome captain than the starfish, since I had seen many starfish in the tide pools of California. Not wanting to dampen his enthusiasm, I feigned curiosity about the creature he presented to me, while stealing glances at those incredible eyes. *Never mind the sea lions, I want to dive right into those twin blue pools.* I hadn't felt attracted to a man in what seemed like ages, and I struggled to remember how to flirt.

After the brief frolic with the sea lions, we made our way to the beach for a picnic lunch and snorkeling. The beauty of the beach and bay reminded me of something on a postcard rack. Creamy sand lined the half-moon bay filled with aquamarine water so clear we could see the bottom a long way from shore. Rocky outcroppings stood sentinel on either end of the beach, with reefs surrounding the island. Lucy and I got right into the water and paddled along in our snorkels and fins, engrossed by the bright-hued parrotfish, angelfish, and Moorish idols pecking at the coral. We eventually returned to the beach for a picnic lunch with the rest of the group, before boarding the boat to return to La Paz.

While Juan was busy with his captain duties on the way back to La Paz, I couldn't stop myself from sneaking glances in his direction. Every now and then Juan smiled my way as he continued to point out interesting sights while we motored back.

All too soon the trip was over and we were back in La Paz. I wanted to find out more about this handsome stranger but didn't have the language skills to strike up a conversation in Spanish. It was time to go and I had nothing to say. *Why didn't I learn more Spanish before I came to Mexico?* I mentally cursed myself. Reluctantly, I shook Juan's hand with a "*Gracias*" and "*Adios*," and Lucy and I walked the stretch of beach back to where our motorhomes were parked. We decided to shower and meet up again for a margarita and dinner.

A few hours later, we wandered over to the cantina near the docks for a "real" Mexican margarita. The cantina was a tiny outdoor bar lined with bar stools. Someone told us we should order a margarita the way the Mexicans drink them, so we did. Apparently, that meant with a lot of liquor. We chatted with the bartender and a couple of locals as we sipped what seemed like a fishbowl of tequila. They taught us a few more words of Spanish, and we all laughed at our terrible pronunciation.

Suddenly, an unmistakable pair of blue eyes appeared on the other side of the bar. I felt a flush of pleasure at this unexpected surprise. Captain Juan was done with his last tour of the day. He remembered us and joined us at the bar for a beer. We struggled to converse in basic Spanish and English, so he ended up chatting more in Spanish with the bartender.

I kept expecting him to leave, perhaps to return to his family, but Juan lingered at the bar until darkness began its descent. I decided it was time for me to head back to my motorhome. I was not drunk but certainly a little bit tipsy and couldn't handle any more "real" margaritas. Juan told me it was "not safe" to walk the beach by myself and, through gestures and broken English, asked if he could walk me to my motorhome. I felt strangely soothed by his gentle nature, and after we'd spent half the day together during the snorkeling excursion, I thought he seemed harmless.

I accepted Juan's offer to escort me up the beach, as Juan expressed frustration over his inability to communicate in English. He claimed it was "*muy importante*" to learn better English. While we walked, I was wondering what I was going to do when we reached my motorhome. It was clear that this handsome and seemingly kind and gentle man was interested in me on some level. I was pretty sure that if I invited him inside, he would accept. But I had never had a one-night stand. I felt the familiar prickling of caution and common sense surfacing. I tried to shove the feeling away—I was not in the mood for caution and common sense. I wanted a vacation romance.

As we neared my door Juan stopped and, in a mixture of Spanish, English, and charades, asked if he could kiss me. I had never been asked that before. Most men just leaned in and, if I didn't back away, started kissing. He was very polite. I smiled, nodded, and inched closer. It was a pleasant surprise to discover that this gorgeous man was also an excellent kisser. The dark cloak of night settled around us and the stars, so brilliant here in Baja, began poking their way through the velvet canopy above.

As we kissed, my conscience and libido battled. *Invite him inside.* I was ready for my dating drought to end.

But what if he's married? He could have a devoted wife and a passel of kids tucked away somewhere.

But he's so handsome.

You can't even talk to him.

I was extremely frustrated by my inability to communicate with Juan. He was handsome and willing, so it would have been so easy to rely on body language as our main form of communication. But since I couldn't find out anything about him through conversation, it just didn't feel right. My conscience won the battle. *Words are so important.*

I thanked him for walking me home, and he made sure I got in my door safely. As I wistfully watched through the window as his dark shape melted into the inky night, I began to wonder if I was the type of person that could have a passionate vacation romance with someone I'd just met. Since I'd just turned away the most handsome and intriguing man I had met in years, I figured I wasn't.

CHAPTER 16

MR. RIGHT NOW

MARCH 2007

Why bother with Mr. Right when Mr. Right Now is gorgeous, available, and asking me to dance?

—Cristiane Serruya

B efore I started my travels, I wasn't looking for Mr. Right. I had given up on that fantasy ages ago. I was too consumed with the darkness of my depression and then the preparations for my motorhome travel to think about dating, and my last relationship was a distant memory. Although I started feeling better when I was preparing to hit the road, I didn't want to get involved with someone just when I was planning to leave the area. I knew from past experience how easily I could be derailed by a guy.

But now, all of the preparations were done and I was living the dream. Time was a plentiful commodity. I was happy, optimistic about my future, and I wanted to play. My experience with Captain Juan told me that I was ready for some romance, without worrying about the future or whether we were soul mates. I didn't want Mr. Right, I wanted Mr. Right Now. I just wanted to be able to communicate with him.

Lucy and I headed south and stopped at an RV park in Los Barriles on our way to Cabo Pulmo. A national marine park, Cabo Pulmo hosts the most northerly coral reefs in the American Pacific. We were anxious to get to the reef and weren't sure whether we wanted to stop in Los Barriles, so we drove into the park, got out of our motorhomes, and wandered around to check it out. We walked past a man standing near a trailer and munching on potato chips, a can of Pringles in his hand. I noticed the potato chips because they were extremely hard to find in Baja. The Mexican stores we had shopped in stocked only tortilla chips.

Men seemed to be at the forefront of my consciousness, because I felt an immediate attraction to this man, although I can't say why. He wasn't especially handsome, but there was an air of quiet confidence about him, without arrogance. He was in his early to mid-fifties, about five foot ten inches tall, with close-cropped hair, glasses, and a friendly smile. There was something sexy yet comfortable about him.

"Are you staying here?" Lucy asked him.

Swallowing his mouthful of potato chips, he said, "Yes, I am. I've been here for a week."

"What do you think of the place?" she asked.

"It's a really nice place to stay. There's a fun group of regulars that come here every winter, and we have lots of social events. I've been coming every year for the past ten years."

Based on his recommendation and our walk around the place, we decided to stay for a night. We checked in, parked our motorhomes, and settled in. Any thoughts of romance were far from my mind when I went to get something from the closet next to the bed and squished across soggy carpet. The Green Monster was up to more mischief.

The water pump was located under the bed, so it didn't take long to figure out why the carpet was wet. It was leaking. Luckily for me, it wasn't a gushing geyser, but rather a seeping drip.

I could see the water oozing from one of the fittings and tried tightening it with a wrench, but nothing seemed loose. I resorted to the universal cure for leaks: I placed a plastic container under the fitting to catch the water. Next, I fetched my owner's manual to see if it contained any useful information to help me out of this predicament. It didn't. I wasn't likely to find an RV repair service in this small town, and plumbing was definitely not my specialty.

I have always been very independent and a bit shy about asking for help, but Lucy was not the least bit shy. After I told her about the leaky pump, she decided to take matters into her own hands. A short time later I was in my motorhome when I heard a knock and opened my door. Outside stood Mr. Potato Chips.

"Hi," he said as he introduced himself. "I heard from your friend that you're having trouble with your water pump. I'm pretty good at fixing things. Would you like me to take a look at it?"

Although I don't like asking for help, I'm always grateful when it shows up on my doorstep. He seemed nice enough, so I thanked him and invited him in to have a look. As I watched this man lying on the floor in the narrow space beside the bed trying to figure out what was wrong with the water pump, I was touched by his willingness to help a perfect stranger in another country. Before I knew it, there were two guys inside my motorhome working on the pump, with three more standing outside the bedroom window making suggestions. They were all friends of my helpful neighbor, who I learned was from Canada.

"Don't you know, it always takes five guys to fix anything," explained the Canadian in a typical northern accent. "One to do the work, and another four to offer advice."

I laughed and made small talk with the guys outside. A half hour later, I still had a leaky water pump with a plastic container beneath it, but I'd made five new friends. There was nothing they could do to fix the pump. Before leaving, the Canadian said, "We're having our weekly bocce ball tournament and happy hour tonight. You and your friend should come."

"Thanks, that sounds fun." I knew Lucy wouldn't pass up a happy hour opportunity, and we had no other plans.

Since I had no cell phone service in Mexico, I walked to the pay phone up the street so that I could call the motorhome manufacturer. The manufacturer put me in touch with the water pump supplier, but this problem couldn't be fixed at the moment. It would have to wait until I returned to California. In the meantime, I had to keep an eye on that plastic container so that it didn't overflow, and also dry out my carpet. I opened the windows so the breeze could flow through the motorhome and aimed my battery-powered fan at the carpet.

At five o'clock, Lucy and I wandered over to watch the bocce ball fun. I met Sandy, a woman from my home state of Minnesota. While I talked with Sandy, I noticed the Canadian hovering nearby, listening in and trying to make conversation. We talked about the sport of curling and winter temperatures that hit twenty below zero—things that only people from the north understand. The Canadian told me he'd flown in from Vancouver and was staying for a few weeks in his friend's travel trailer, which was left there all year.

It turned out the Canadian and his friends were amateur winemakers. This was welcome news, since it was nearly impossible to find decent wine in Baja. Later, Lucy and I were sitting in her motorhome having a glass of Baja wine, which tasted like something used to clean the bathroom, when there was a knock on the door. It was the Canadian with Tom and Pete, two of his friends who'd tried to help with the water pump. Tom and Pete were also in their fifties and had the hallmark of middle age: a few extra pounds around the middle.

"We thought you might like some of our homemade wine, and an appetizer."

We eyed the bottles of homemade wine and the plateful of fresh-looking tomatoes covered with mozzarella cheese and drizzled with balsamic, and enthusiastically invited them in. While one of them opened the wine, Lucy and I were happy to toss the bathroom cleaner from our glasses. They filled our glasses instead with some tasty Zinfandel and passed around the appetizers.

The three men had been good friends for many years. They were all still working, but since Canadians get more vacation time than Americans do, they were able to spend weeks together in Los Barriles every year and still have vacation time left over. They knew a lot about the area and soon were passing on helpful tidbits sprinkled liberally with jokes. We were having such a good time that I barely noticed when one of the men went back to their RV to get more wine. Our glasses were refilled as soon as they were empty. We ended up talking and laughing into the wee hours with our new northern friends. In fact, we were having so much fun that some fellow campers knocked on the door and asked us to keep it down when it got too late. We shushed each other and giggled as we shut the windows and doors so we wouldn't disturb our neighbors.

"Where are you headed next?" Pete asked.

"Cabo Pulmo," Lucy said. "We're leaving tomorrow to go see the reef."

"So soon?" the Canadian asked. Then he looked at me. "You just got here. Why don't you stay here for a few days? There's a lot to do here. It's a fun group. Isn't that right?" He looked at his buddies.

"Oh yeah, really fun group," Tom said. "We play bocce and have happy hour every Friday."

"We have potlucks, too," chimed in Pete. "And some of us go biking together."

"We take the boat out or drive into town—there's always something going on," the Canadian added.

"Sounds fun," Lucy said. "What do you think, Heidi? Do you want to stay here a few days?"

"Fine with me. I'm in no rush."

The Canadian smiled. As the night wore on, he became increasingly flirtatious and complimentary. He was charming and funny, and very comfortable to be around. I liked him. There had always been something about men who made me laugh that I found irresistible.

Lucy and I were sitting at the booth in the kitchen facing the men, who were scattered around the living area. I was sitting sideways in the booth with my arm resting along the top of it. The Canadian was sitting on the sofa next to me. "I'm really glad you're staying," he said in a low voice, running his index finger lightly along my forearm.

I was surprised at the bold intimacy but couldn't help noticing the tingle of electricity traveling the trail of his touch. It was startling how delicious a light fingertip felt on hungry skin. My cheeks flushed, but I didn't pull my arm away.

We laughed and talked until four in the morning, and I couldn't remember the last time I'd stayed up that late—or drunk that much wine. Although the evening was the most raucous fun I'd experienced since arriving in Baja, I needed some sleep. The Canadian insisted on escorting me to my door, although it wasn't far. He was clearly hoping for an invitation to come inside. Although I found something very sexy about this man who made me laugh and had a delicate yet electric touch, I wasn't ready to invite him inside. Not yet.

CHAPTER 17

ROMANCE

MARCH 2007

Romance is the glamour which turns the dust of everyday life into a golden haze.

—Elinor Glyn

A t ten a.m. the next morning, the Canadian was knocking at my door. "Would you like to go for a bike ride?" he asked, pointing to the Mount Everest-looking hill nearby. "I have an extra bike you can use."

I groaned inwardly. I wasn't quite ready to face the day after too much wine and not enough sleep, and I definitely wasn't ready to climb Mount Everest. *Why are men so often in a hurry?* I needed some time to process my feelings about this man, so I thanked him for the invitation and suggested we meet up later. Then I crawled back into bed.

We caught up with each other later that day in the "internet café." This was a shaded area next to one of the RVs with tables and chairs, where, for a small fee, people in the park could get the password for the secure Wi-Fi connection and check email. Over the next few days, the Canadian and I met up here and there. We shared some walks and good conversation, getting to know each other better.

"So, what's your story?" I asked. "Are you married, do you have kids?"

"I'm divorced, and I don't have any kids. What about you?"

"I'm divorced too, and I have a twenty-one-year-old daughter back in California."

He seemed kind, gentle, and as if he was a romantic like me. Although he wasn't movie-star handsome like Captain Juan, I found myself becoming more attracted to him. His rugged sexiness made him appealing, but it was his charm that really hooked me. His frequent compliments made me feel appreciated, but they seemed genuine, not like pickup lines. He also seemed very curious about me, and asked lots of questions about my life in California and why I decided to hit the road.

The night before Lucy and I planned to leave for Cabo Pulmo, the Canadian came over to my motorhome to say goodbye, offering a bottle of wine for the road. I decided I was tired of my romance drought. I knew we would probably never see each other again, but I didn't care. He'd offered to help me in my time of need, we'd shared many laughs, and he'd made me feel appreciated. The Canadian was Mr. Right Now. I invited him in for a glass of wine. As the bottle emptied, the space between us disappeared. First it was a light touch, then a kiss, a caress, and our clothing melted away. My starving skin responded to every little touch, and I greedily feasted on this pleasure banquet without hesitation or shyness. Later, when we were saying goodbye, he asked, "Would it be okay if I join you in Cabo Pulmo for a few days?"

I was surprised. Cabo Pulmo is located about an hour south from Los Barriles. I figured maybe that was his way of avoiding an awkward goodbye. "Sure," I said casually, not really expecting him to show up. *He's on vacation with his buddies; he's not likely to drive to Cabo Pulmo for a few days with me.* As we kissed goodbye, I figured that was the last I would see of the Canadian, but I was okay with that. We'd enjoyed each other for a few days, and the desert landscape of my romantic life had transformed into an oasis, if only for a short time.

The next day, Lucy and I hit the road for Cabo Pulmo. When we arrived, we parked our motorhomes on a dirt road next to a tiny cabana-style restaurant by the beach. There was a handful of tables on a covered patio with a view of the cobalt sea. It was not far from where the fishing pangas pulled in with their catch of the day. The reef was a moderate swim just offshore. Small palapas lined the beach to provide shade, but the beach was nearly empty. It was another perfect postcard shot.

I told Lucy the Canadian had asked if he could join me for a few days.

"Don't worry," I said. "He won't show up."

"Oh, he'll show up," Lucy said with certainty.

After spending some time on the beach, we showered and were heading to the restaurant for dinner when I saw a dated blue pickup pulling up next to the motorhomes. It was the Canadian, in the truck he'd borrowed from Tom. I felt a jumbled rush of surprise, pleasure, and then awkwardness.

"You were right," I said to Lucy. "He did show up." I wondered if she would be upset. My awkward feelings soon disappeared as the Canadian charmed not only me but Lucy as well, over delicious margaritas and the best sea bass dinner I have ever tasted. The company might have had something to do with my enjoyment.

The woman who ran the restaurant cooked up whatever her husband caught each day on his fishing trip. She also shared the secrets to her delicious margaritas: lots of fresh limes, good tequila, Fresca, and Damiana. The last ingredient was a liqueur that came in a bottle shaped like a plump naked woman. The restaurant owner insisted Damiana was an aphrodisiac. It was a claim we would hear repeatedly on this trip. It must have been true, because the next few days seemed like pages stolen from a romance novel.

The Canadian was generous and thoughtful. He brought me little gifts—matching wine and water glasses, expensive food treats from Canada, and of course, homemade wine. He also brought Pringles potato chips. He massaged my feet with scented lotion he'd brought. It was so over-the-top, I wondered if I was dreaming. He seemed solely focused on pleasing me. This was a kind of seduction I had never experienced before, and I was more than willing to participate. I responded with an openness, affection, and playfulness I had tucked away for a very long time.

The Canadian tried to learn everything about me: what I liked and didn't like, and what gave me pleasure. Especially what gave me pleasure. He studied my body like a musician studies his instrument, learning every curve and hollow, and how to get the best reaction. He was a tireless lover of foreplay, and he examined the responses of my body just as intently as he searched my mind. I had never before experienced such attention and pleasure. It was intoxicating. In return, I unleashed all of my pent-up passion, playfulness, and appreciation on him. We laughed and enjoyed every minute of each other. For once, I was living totally in the moment, not worrying about the future, and loving it.

One day we decided to hike to a secluded cove called Mermaid Rock, named for a rock formation that looked like a mermaid sitting on her tail. To get there, we walked along a narrow trail perched on a high bluff, paying careful attention to our footing so we didn't fall over the edge. Without my asking, the Canadian took the bag I was carrying with my beach towel, water, and other items, so I could concentrate on my footing. He was always a gentleman and on the lookout for ways to help me.

When we arrived at Mermaid Rock we had the place to ourselves. There was a tiny semi-enclosed bay right next to the rock, where the water was warmer. We kissed and frolicked in the water, enjoying the solitude. Just as the passion was heating up, we were interrupted by a tour boat that pulled up near the shore to see the famous Mermaid Rock. We took one look at the tourists with their poised cameras, laughed, and decided we should find a lesser-known location. We moved away from the rock and, after a snack on the beach, returned to the motorhome to meet up with Lucy for some snorkeling.

We put on our snorkeling gear and started swimming to the reef with Lucy. We swam along the reef, but the deeper water was cold, the fish were few, and the visibility was poor. We told Lucy we were heading to the beach, and I left the water shivering. We spread our towels on the sand and lay down to warm ourselves. As I lay on my stomach with my eyes closed, the Canadian ran his finger down my bare spine, and I felt every nerve in my body jump to attention. Mr. Right Now had a magic touch.

"*Bella*," he said softly as he looked at me.

"What did you say?" I couldn't make out what he'd said.

"*Bella*. It means 'beautiful' in Italian. You're beautiful."

"Aren't you a charmer," I said with a smile as I wrapped my arms around him and gave him a kiss. "Whatever you're doing, it's working."

He wanted to know not only about me, but also about my family, old boyfriends—all of the little details of my life. "What were you like as a child?" he asked. "Who is your best friend? What's your favorite color?"

I learned a few things about his life. His mother had died years ago, his dad was getting frail, and he was close to his sister and her family. But usually when I asked questions about him and his life, the conversation seemed to end up back on me.

One day we were walking along the beach on our way to swim when he put his arms around me, drew me close, and looked deeply into my eyes. "I have never felt so alive," he said, smiling at me. "You make me feel so young and happy. I would tell you that I love you, but it would be too soon, wouldn't it?"

"Yes," I agreed. "Too soon. We don't really even know each other yet." But inside and out, I was smiling. The communication struggles I'd had with Captain Juan were nonexistent with the Canadian. Not only did we speak the same language, but he seemed very willing to talk and express his feelings.

Although I hadn't known him long and we were staying together in a small space, he was very easy to be with. He woke up early each morning, so he took Rylie for a walk. I appreciated the break from this daily duty and enjoyed sleeping in.

One day he looked at me and said, "I'm so lucky. That day you walked into the Los Barriles RV park was a really good day for me. Can I have your email address? I'd like to write to you when I'm back in Canada. Would that be okay?" This was the first hint of reality that crept into my romantic fantasy. He was on vacation, and soon he would be returning to work.

"That would be more than okay." I wrote down my email address and gave it to him. I wasn't ready yet to think about his leaving.

"What is your favorite movie?" he asked later that day.

"*Out of Africa* with Meryl Streep and Robert Redford. It's beautiful, romantic, and incredibly sad. I have it, do you want to watch it?"

He did. We spooned on the couch together as we watched the movie. I pointed out some of my favorite scenes, like when Robert Redford's character is washing Meryl Streep's hair and reciting poetry, and when they are flying in an airplane with a huge flock of birds and beautiful scenery below them, and she reaches back to hold his hand.

Every day we walked with Rylie along the beach with its straw-covered palapas, and we met Lucy every evening for lively catch-of-the-day dinners. I had been craving romance, and now it was gushing from a fire hose.

This man was the Mr. Right Now that I wanted. He awakened something in me that had been dormant for quite some time—that playful, romantic part of myself that needed the freedom of time and travel to emerge. I was finally feeling comfortable in my own skin, and that skin wanted to be touched. Although I knew it wasn't likely that we would see each other after this visit, I couldn't help but feel some attachment to this man after so much intimacy and fun. Despite my better judgment, I was falling in love. I was falling hard.

Shortly before the Canadian planned to leave, I was standing in the kitchen, cutting up vegetables for our last meal together. He was sitting on the sofa with a glass of wine talking with me while I chopped.

"Heidi," he said quietly. "I need to tell you something."

"Yes, what is it?" I looked up from my chopping, but my smile faded when I saw the grim look on his face. "What's wrong?"

"I haven't been totally honest with you. I'm married."

CHAPTER 18

FALLING FROM CLOUD NINE

MARCH 2007

*Our greatest glory is not in never falling, but in rising
every time we fall.*

—Confucius

S tunned, I couldn't speak for a few moments. I felt as
though the world had stopped, but when I looked down,
my hands were still chopping vegetables. Apparently, they
didn't know my heart had just shattered into pieces at my feet.
The years of pretending nothing was wrong in my family had
trained me not to react when the rug was pulled out from
under me. *Stiff upper lip. Don't make a scene.* I put the knife
down. After an eternity of silence that was only moments, I
finally managed to choke out some words.

"But you told me you were divorced." I looked at him in
confusion.

"We basically live separate lives," he said hastily. "We might
as well be divorced. We never do anything together."

I remembered the men I'd encountered during my travels
who pretended they were single or separated from their wives
when they really weren't. *How did I not see it this time?* "You
mean you haven't even filed for divorce?"

"Not exactly. We have some things to work out first."

The cells inside my body were crumbling, turning to dust, and I wanted to be anywhere other than in that moment. *How could he lie to me like that?* I always tried to be really honest with everyone, and I expected others to be honest with me. Knowing that I'd believed everything this man had told me when it was apparently all a calculated performance left me feeling heartbroken and humiliated. *Fooled by a married man.*

I'd known women over the years who got involved with married men, but I'd never understood it. In my book, it was wrong. People could get hurt, families torn apart. Why would anyone fall for a married man when there was no possibility of a future together? I had certainly never thought I would get involved with one. I thought I was smarter than that. Usually, I was. My mind spun back through the days since we'd met. *What clues did I miss? Where did I go wrong?* Even though I'd believed his lie about being divorced, somehow, I felt responsible and guilty.

"I should have known," was all I could say. I remembered the old saying "If something seems too good to be true, it usually is." All of the attention, appreciation, and romance was so over-the-top, I should have known there was a catch. I felt the storybook romance of the past week unraveling like a handmade sweater. I blamed myself as much as I blamed him. *I should have questioned him more thoroughly. I shouldn't have gotten involved with him so soon. I should have seen the signs.*

I should have kicked him out immediately. A different person might have been screaming and smashing dishes against the wall—maybe even throwing that chopping knife. But in my family, we didn't make a scene. I didn't have violent outbursts. I was the stoic, always remaining calm during a crisis, stuffing my feelings and maintaining my composure until the catastrophe was over. Then I fell apart later when I finally allowed myself to feel. But now I just felt confused and paralyzed.

Somehow, I got through the rest of our time together. I wanted him to leave so I could be alone to process my confused feelings. As I watched him get in his truck and drive off, I felt a mixture of relief and sadness. I wanted this man out of my sight, and yet, part of me wanted to hang on to the romance we'd shared together. I thought I'd finally found what was missing for so long, and I wasn't ready to let go of the fantasy. I wanted to believe all of the wonderful things he'd said.

The next day, Lucy and I left Cabo Pulmo to head south. As I drove away from the beach I watched in the mirror as the dust left behind swirled into the air, taking my beautiful memories with it. We drove around Southern Baja during our final two weeks in Mexico, stopping briefly in Cabo San Lucas and Todos Santos. I sang along to brokenhearted music and cried, playing the same sad songs over and over. I don't know if it was the loss of the person that I mourned or the belief in the romantic dream. The Canadian had delivered more than I ever expected—or hoped for—but it was all just a memory now. I reminded myself that I was only looking for Mr. Right Now, and right now had come and gone.

On our way back north, Lucy and I couldn't resist another stop at El Coyote Beach to see Frankie and Stan again, who stayed there every winter. They warned us we might want to consider crossing back into the US before Easter, because many locals were off work around Easter week, and the beaches got very noisy and crowded. After talking it over, we decided to cross the border with Frankie and Stan, who were also headed back to the States.

A few days later our three-motorhome caravan stopped for a night at San Ignacio. We walked around town and discovered a dance festival in the plaza, with children from preschool age through high school performing traditional dances. We joined the crowd and enjoyed the dancers, their bright outfits a swirl of cheerful color that lifted my spirits, if only for a while.

The next morning, we were preparing to leave the campground to continue north when we heard Lucy's distressed voice calling us. "I can't find Joe," she wailed. "He got out of the motorhome and I can't find him anywhere."

Joe was Lucy's cat. He was entirely black, except for a white star on his chest, and in typical cat fashion was good at disappearing when he felt like it. The four of us searched the campground, calling Joe's name. We went to the office and asked the campground manager if he had seen a black cat wandering around. He hadn't.

"I know he'll come back when it's time to eat," Lucy said. "He always does."

I looked at Frankie and Stan, who seemed anxious to leave. "Why don't you two head north? I'll stay here with Lucy and look for Joe. We can join you at Los Angeles Bay." We were all planning to spend a few days there before crossing the border.

"No, Heidi, you should go ahead with Frankie and Stan. I'll catch up with you later," Lucy protested.

"No way, I'm not leaving you here alone. We'll look for Joe together."

"Oh, thank you, Heidi!" Lucy said gratefully. She went looking in one direction, while I went in the other. After a thorough search of the campground and the surrounding area with no luck, we decided to take a break. About an hour later, I heard Lucy calling from her motorhome.

"He's back!" Just as she'd said, Joe came back to eat. She quickly grabbed him and put him safely in the motorhome. We got ready and hit the road.

Bahía de los Ángeles, or Los Angeles Bay, was a short distance off Highway 1 on the Sea of Cortez. We met up with Frankie and Stan at the designated campground. The sun glittered on the brilliant blue bay, which was spotted with small, rocky islands. We talked as we walked the area, drinking it all in. The next day, we went out exploring in Frankie and Stan's Jeep.

As we were driving around, we came across an American, Leon, who was standing near a house not far from the bay. He waved and greeted us through the open windows as though we were good friends. He was a friendly, talkative guy, and soon he was inviting us in for a beer and some smoked fish. We learned that Leon had bought the house and lived there full-time. He said there were many Americans doing the same thing, because it was so expensive to live in America and so cheap in Mexico. The American dream of home ownership and financial security didn't seem to be working so well for many Americans, especially in expensive areas like California. I considered whether I could live in Mexico. I decided that as much as I loved visiting, I couldn't see myself living there full-time at this point in my life. Two months was long enough, and I was ready to return to the States. I missed Cammie.

We drove to the border and were eventually allowed to enter the United States by the stern-faced border patrol after a thorough check of our motorhomes. I noticed how much more difficult it was to cross the border going north than it was going south. America was not as welcoming as Mexico. I felt a wave of sadness roll over me as I left my carefree life on the beach behind but comforted myself with the thought that I still had five months left in my year of freedom.

Lucy and I decided to stay for a few days at a pretty campground not far from the border. It sported a large pond dotted with ducks and geese, grassy campsites, and lacy shade trees. We both needed to catch up on some things, and I needed to deal with my leaky water pump. I was back in the US only a few days when the email arrived.

CHAPTER 19

THE EMAIL

APRIL 2007

*Labor to keep alive in your breast that little spark of
celestial fire called conscience.*

—George Washington

I stared at the Canadian's name in my email, my heart
pounding. I remembered giving him my email address, but I
didn't think he would contact me after telling me he was
married.

I knew I should immediately delete the email without
reading it, but romance is a very powerful drug. Memories of
the beautiful things he'd said to me, swimming at Mermaid
Beach, and the laughs we'd shared danced through my head. I
relived the happiness and passion of those days we'd spent
together and how he made me feel. I struggled with my
conscience and jumbled feelings as I wavered between deleting
and opening the email. I remembered how I'd felt when he told
me he was married, and how my romantic dream had shattered
like a broken window. The pain of that moment filled my eyes
and I turned away from the laptop.

I swiped at my overflowing tears with the back of my hand
and flopped onto the sofa, suddenly feeling exhausted. I turned

on the TV and flipped through the channels in search of a movie to distract me. Suddenly, an image of Robert Redford appeared on the screen. It was the scene where he is pouring water onto Meryl Streep's head, washing her hair as he recited poetry. The movie was *Out of Africa*. I couldn't believe it. That was the movie we'd watched together, our limbs braided. *What kind of cruel joke is this?*

As I watched the movie, I remembered all of the laughter we'd shared and the sweet things he'd told me, and a fresh batch of tears rolled down my cheeks. I grabbed my laptop, pushed my conscience aside, took a deep breath, and opened the email. It was a long epistle of apology, full of regret, and asking forgiveness.

"I should have been up front with you," he wrote. "But I knew if I told you I was married, you wouldn't have anything to do with me. I didn't want to lose my chance with you. I told you my wife and I basically live separate lives, and that's true." The email went on to tell me how our time together had awakened something in him and how much he cared for me. Toward the end of the email he asked, "Can you ever forgive me?"

I stared at this question for a long time. *Can I forgive him? Do I want to forgive him? If they're living separate lives, does that mean he's getting a divorce?* I wanted to believe that he was, but I didn't trust him.

I knew that I shouldn't respond to the email, but now I wanted to say all of the things I hadn't said when he dropped his news bomb because I was too stunned and needed time to process things. I have never been fast on my feet and usually need to analyze things before I speak. Now that I'd had time to think about what happened, I wanted him to know that what he'd done to me was wrong and how he'd hurt me. At least that was what I told myself, but if I were really honest with myself, I would have admitted that my heart was still clutching the tattered cloth of the romantic dream, refusing to let it go. I wavered as my conscience and heart battled it out. *It's not as though I'll see him again, it's just an email.* I hit the reply button.

The color rose in my cheeks as I furiously typed, the hurt feelings fueling my fingers. I ranted and raved a bit, then ended with, "I have no interest in getting involved with a married man. Have a good life." I wiped the tears from my eyes as I hit the send button, and the romantic dream I had nurtured in Baja floated away on the internet waves. This reopened the wound, and it felt as though a hole had been ripped in the pocket of my heart and something precious had fallen out.

Chapter 20

Hoodoos and Arches

April 2007

*The biggest adventure you can take is to live the life of
your dreams.*

—Oprah Winfrey

I pushed my anger and grief aside as much as I could and
focused on my plans. I spent the next week in the Los
Angeles area, visiting with Cindy for a couple of days at her
sister's house and then spending time with Cammie. She flew
down from the Bay Area to celebrate her twenty-second
birthday with me at Disneyland. We had celebrated her
birthday at Disneyland every three years from the time she was
three until she turned fifteen. Her fifteenth birthday was
celebrated in Cancún, and then three years later we went to
France for a combined birthday and high school graduation
celebration. For this birthday, she wanted to return to
Disneyland again, and I was eager to see her and repeat the old
birthday tradition.

We laughed until our faces hurt as we spun around like
tops in the teacup ride and squealed at the surprises of A Bug's
Land. Space Mountain had always been my favorite ride, and
we sped around in the dark again and again, until the fun wore

us out. This precious mother-daughter time fed my heart and soul.

"I've really missed you," I told her.

"I missed you too, Mom. But I'm glad you're having such a good time."

I could see she was happy and doing well, and I felt less guilty about leaving her to pursue my travels. Too soon, it was time for her to return to work, and I had some more traveling to do. I planned to spend the rest of April and early May exploring some of the national parks in Utah as well as the Grand Canyon, all new places for me.

With Cammie gone and no longer the focus of my attention, I found unwelcome thoughts of the Canadian creeping into my head. I pushed them out of my mind as best I could and tried to concentrate on my trip. The beauty and wonder of the national parks turned out to be a great distraction.

After leaving the Los Angeles area I drove for two days, then stopped in Barstow, California. I planned to stay at a Bureau of Land Management campground nearby. After discovering the directions in my BLM campground book were useless and driving around aimlessly for what seemed like hours, I asked three people in town where it was. None of them knew, so I decided to stay at the Ghost Town Campground in Calico, instead. There was a fierce wind and the temperatures were bone-rattlingly cold.

"How much do I owe you?" I asked the ranger at the entrance as I got out my wallet.

"Take any spot that's available. You can pay the eighteen dollars to the camp host tomorrow morning. He'll come by between eight and nine," she said as she quickly shut the window to her booth. She looked miserable, huddled in her parka.

I found the only level campsite I could find at the end of the campground, grateful that I didn't have to go out in the cold to use my leveling blocks. There were no hookups at this bare-bones site, but I didn't need them. The wind was a blustery force that squelched any lengthy outdoor activities. Other than a few short walks with Rylie and a hurried walk through Calico, I didn't do much outside. The next morning, I waited until nine thirty a.m., but no one came to collect my eighteen dollars. I wandered around but couldn't find any sign of a park ranger. The ranger shack was deserted. I had a long day of driving ahead of me, so finally I decided to leave. I tried to find someone to give my camping fee to on my way out of the campground, with no luck. There was no box in which to deposit it, so I left, feeling like a criminal. I watched the rearview mirror as I drove off, expecting to see flashing red lights behind me. None appeared.

I drove to Springdale, Utah, just outside of Zion National Park, and spent the night. The next morning, I moved to the South Campground inside the park. The campground was surrounded on all sides by towering scarlet rocks, and the gurgling Virgin River curled alongside it. *Majestic* was the first word that came to mind as I took in the Zion scenery, cliché though it was.

It rained every day except one while I was there, but I managed to squeeze in a few short hikes. Rylie and I walked the easy Pa'rus Trail, because it was the only trail that allowed dogs. I hiked the Weeping Rock and Emerald Pools Trails, and part of the Riverside Walk, the hood of my rain jacket pulled low on my forehead against the spitting rain. As I hiked, my mind kept wandering back to the Canadian. I replayed the events, trying to make peace with what had happened. I got nowhere.

On the day I planned to leave Zion, I was told there were bad road conditions in either direction. Freezing rain and then snow were making for very nasty driving. I decided to stay an extra day. I paid more attention to driving conditions when I was driving the motorhome than I did when driving my car.

A light powdering of snow on the peak of the rock cliffs and a sharp chill in the air reminded me that it was still early in the season, especially at this elevation. *I'll have to come back later in the season when the weather is better.*

After leaving the park I followed State Route 9 through the Zion-Mount Carmel Tunnel. It was a squat and narrow tunnel, so there were vehicle size restrictions that were closely monitored. Recreational vehicles had to be measured to make sure they fell below the height and width limitations, and a special permit was required for vehicles that exceeded them. Park rangers at either end stopped the traffic coming in the opposite direction to allow large vehicles with permits to pass through. When it was my turn, I nervously straddled the orange line in the middle of the lanes as I drove the motorhome through the tunnel. The drive on Route 9 was full of hairpin turns, but the beauty of the scenery I glimpsed when I could briefly tear my eyes away from the road was well worth the knuckle-biting journey. I wished that Rylie could drive, so I could have seen more of it.

I meandered up Highway 89 to Highway 12 and eventually entered Bryce Canyon National Park. At the first viewing area, I parked the motorhome and walked to the overlook to get my first glimpse. When I gazed into the valley below me, I thought I was on Mars. The rock formations, called hoodoos, were like cinnamon-and-salmon-colored goblins filling the valley. I itched to get down into that otherworldly landscape, but it had to wait for another day. It was getting late, and I had to get settled into a campsite.

I climbed back into the motorhome and drove to the campground. Enormous pine trees towered over it, creating large shadows lingering on snowbanks. The snarling wind added to the inhospitable atmosphere, and there was no Wi-Fi. I checked my campground book and discovered there was another campground nearby, so I headed down the highway to check out Kodachrome Basin State Park.

This park was about a half hour from Bryce, at a lower elevation, and much less crowded. The weather was warmer here, the sun brightened the campground, and there was no snow. The campground was much prettier, flanked by striped rock towers forming interesting shapes. It also had Wi-Fi, which was always an added bonus. This seemed like a good home base for exploring the area while I waited for the weather in Bryce to clear.

The nicest thing about Kodachrome was that, since it was a state park and not a national park, dogs were allowed on the hiking trails. I took Rylie with me as I hiked around the park, and he loved it. We walked the Shakespeare Arch and Angel's Palace trails, where rabbits scampered all around us, more plentiful than squirrels in California. This was every dog's greatest fantasy. In an excited delirium, Rylie took off like a shot every few minutes, forgetting about the leash tethered to his collar. I worried he might strangle himself or hurt his neck, but it didn't seem to faze him.

One afternoon, I drove to Grosvenor Arch in Grand Staircase-Escalante National Monument. This was a huge area with stark, deserted-looking scenery, and I drove for miles without seeing another soul or any sign of civilization. Even though I had Rylie with me in the car, this desolate landscape made me feel incredibly lonely and vulnerable. I felt a prickly sense of uneasiness, although I can't say why. Maybe it was because I had never spent so much time without any sign of another human. I didn't like it. I like solitude, but this was a lonely—almost eerie—feeling. The sun was setting, and after visiting the arch, I was ready to head back to the relative civilization of the Kodachrome campground. As I was driving the long, lonely road, I was relieved to see a pair of headlights approaching. *I am not alone!*

After exploring Kodachrome and Escalante, I checked the weather report. The conditions had improved, and it was time to visit Bryce. I drove the length of the park my first day there, stopping at many of the viewing areas. It seemed each was more incredible than the last. I decided on a hiking trail for the following day and drove back to Kodachrome for the night.

After getting Rylie walked and fed the next morning, I made sure he had what he needed for the day. Because Bryce was a national park and didn't allow dogs, I had to leave him behind in the motorhome. I always felt a little bit nervous doing this. I usually told my mom when I was planning to do a hike on my own, just in case something happened to me on the trail. I didn't want Rylie to be stuck in the motorhome alone if something terrible happened to me, like those dachshunds at the Albuquerque balloon fiesta. That had made quite an impression on me. I always made sure he had plenty of food and water and walked him before I left.

I drove the half hour back to Bryce, to the Queens Garden trailhead. As wonderful as the rock formations had looked from the rim, they were even more astonishing once I got down among them. I felt like a dwarf next to friendly, towering giants. As I was descending into the canyon, I came upon three men who were taking photos of each other in front of some towering rock formations.

"Would you like me to take your photo?" I asked.

"That would be great," they responded. They put their arms around each other and grinned at the camera. I took a few shots and handed back their camera. Then one of them asked, "Would you like a picture of yourself?"

"Okay," I said, reluctant to get in front of the camera. I always feel a bit self-conscious being photographed, but when I saw the photo later, I was glad I did. I looked happy and at ease standing in front of the dramatic orange hoodoos. It made me realize that I really did feel more confident now. Although I had done things that many people considered brave, like moving to another state when I didn't know a soul and taking off for a year in a motorhome, I'd suffered from bouts of insecurity throughout my life. This motorhome experience was making me self-assured, as well as creating some incredible memories.

"Enjoy your hike," I called over my shoulder as I headed down the trail. I felt a sense of camaraderie with these fellow hikers, and we joked as we ran into each other a few times during stops along the trail.

The three-mile hike was fairly short, but it was pretty steep hoofing it back out of the canyon. At one point, the trail was not clearly marked, and I took a wrong turn. I started climbing a difficult, rocky canyon. As I tried to scramble up the loose boulders, I realized I must have made a wrong turn somewhere. The terrain was too tricky, and it just didn't feel right. I turned around and retraced my steps, finding the trail before I got myself into trouble.

The early May sun had been shining brilliantly as I began my hike and descended into the canyon. I had taken off my rain jacket and was wearing short sleeves. As I trudged slowly up the steep wall back to the top, the clouds sidled in, the wind started huffing, and large nuggets of rain began pelting me. I was grateful for the rain jacket I had tied around my waist once I warmed up. I put it back on. As I was heading toward the parking lot, the rain transformed to sleet. By the time I reached my car, it was snow. *Spring weather changes quickly in Utah!* I was relieved that I was not in the middle of my hike with miles yet to travel.

I climbed into my car and triumphantly slammed the door shut. *I just barely beat the weather!* I'd just completed a hike alone in a strange place for the first time, and it felt good. Although I had done many things on my own, including raising a child, moving to new states, and setting out on a cross-country travel adventure, I had not done much solo hiking before. Somehow, this felt different. It was a new experience that had unfamiliar territory and physical challenges, and I had only myself to rely on. I felt happy that I could enjoy this activity without fear and not feel like there was something wrong or lacking because I wasn't part of a couple or a group.

This was another turning point for me. I let go of some of the insecurity I had carried with me most of my life about being single—alone. I realized that I could rely on my own wits, common sense, intuition, and sense of adventure. I didn't need anyone else to guide me or complete me. I was happy just doing what I wanted on my own. I felt myself growing stronger, happier, and more self-assured.

I had one more park I wanted to see before getting to Arizona, and that was Arches National Park. Highway 12 is touted as one of the most scenic highways in America, and I have to agree. There were no mousy landscapes on this drive. This was the red-rock-dotted Wild West. It was amazing how quickly the scenery changed, and it was all so dramatic.

Silly me, I thought I could waltz into Arches National Park and the campground would welcome me with open arms. I didn't realize that people were lining up at six a.m. to get the few campsites that became available. After an excruciating wait in a long line of cars to get to the entrance station to the park and the campground, I finally got to talk to a ranger.

"Sorry, the campground is full," the ranger said. "There's an antique car show going on in Moab, plus a four-wheeling convention, so the park campgrounds are full."

"Do you know where I might be able to find a campsite?" I asked.

"You can try Big Bend campground," the ranger offered. She gave me directions to the campground.

I drove to the nearby town of Moab and then to the Big Bend campground. I was very lucky to nab one of the last campsites that could accommodate an RV. The campground was perched on the banks of the Colorado River, just outside of Arches. This was a Bureau of Land Management campground, which are known to have fewer amenities. There were no hookups, but the pretty canyon scenery and $10-per-night price tag made it a no-brainer. The river gurgled softly nearby as I lay in bed at night, the sweetest lullaby there is.

After a night of blissful sleep, I walked and fed Rylie, then headed to Arches for a day of hiking. I did a series of short hikes, including Landscape Arch, Skyline Arch, the Windows, and Balanced Rock. The weather here was very hot, and quite a contrast to the weather in Zion and Bryce. The more solo hikes I took, the more I enjoyed them, and the better I felt about myself. Although there were definitely times when I wished I had a companion to share the beauty surrounding me, I became more at peace with my solo status. I also think I met more people on the trail than I would have if I had been engrossed in conversation with a companion.

After a couple of days, it was time to head to Arizona for the granddaddy of national parks: the Grand Canyon. This park was high on my bucket list, and I couldn't wait to see it.

CHAPTER 21

THE GRANDEST CANYON

MAY 2007

I learned that courage was not the absence of fear, but the triumph over it.

—Nelson Mandela

I woke up with a start, excited, when I realized what I was doing that day. *I'm seeing the Grand Canyon!* It was another dream come true for me, and I couldn't wait to see it. I drove into the park and stopped at the nearest overlook to get my first glimpse of the canyon. As I speed-walked to the viewing point, Rylie had to hustle to keep up with me—usually it was the other way around. The distant ribbon of the Colorado River curled along the stripes of gray, green, and salmon of the canyon walls as far as I could see. The vastness and the incredible art of nature caused a lump in my throat, and I could see why the Native Americans considered it a very sacred place. I found a bench to lounge on for a while to absorb it all, my entire body flooded with emotion. *I am so happy. What if I had given up before I ever got to see this place?*

I had a similar feeling when I first walked along the rim trail. I had to keep stopping and snapping pictures, or simply drinking it in with thirsty eyes. In my excitement to see the canyon, I forgot about Rylie, who was following along at the other end of the leash. All of a sudden, he jumped up onto one of the stone walls that separated the trail from the very long drop into the canyon below. *He's going over the edge!*

Panicked, I made a grab for him, then realized that he was not diving into the canyon but just wanted to hop onto the wall to see what I was gawking at. I picked him up so that he could have a good look from the safety of my arms. He seemed pretty interested in it for a minute or two, and then he was done.

The following morning, we were walking a different portion of the rim trail when a chipmunk darted across the trail toward the canyon. Rylie took off after it like a shot. I was holding tightly on to the retractable leash, but it was not securely latched onto his collar, so when it finished unspooling, I found myself holding an empty leash. Rylie continued racing toward the canyon after the chipmunk. I had already seen those chipmunks dive over the edge of the canyon at top speed. I didn't know how they survived it without tumbling to the canyon floor, but a dog would not. Rylie, who had been deprived of chasing dozens of rabbits and squirrels on this trip, finally found himself free to race after his escaping prey, which he did with great gusto. *He's really going over the edge this time!*

"Rylie, no!" I shouted as I ran after him. Never very good at responding to commands when he wanted a chase, he kept running as fast as his legs would move. "Rylie, leave it!" I shouted louder, hoping this command would produce better results. Still he kept running. My heart was racing triple time, and I felt a surge of adrenaline rush through my veins, but still I couldn't catch him. By this time, he was almost to the edge of the canyon. I took a breath and screamed, "Rylie, no!" Finally, he stopped, just before the edge. I nearly cried with relief, and quickly caught him and fastened the leash with trembling fingers. I made sure it was snapped on tightly and made a mental note to buy a new one the first chance I got. We were done walking near the rim, but it took a long time for the adrenaline surge to disappear.

It takes most people two days to hike to the bottom of the Grand Canyon and back up, so as much as I wanted to, I wasn't doing that on this trip. I couldn't leave Rylie that long, and he wasn't allowed to come with me on the trails. That meant doing short hikes part of the way down the canyon. I decided to hike the Bright Angel Trail one day and the South Kaibab Trail the next. The Kaibab Trail was steeper than the Bright Angel Trail, but there were much fewer people on it, which was nice. It was also narrower than the Bright Angel Trail, which makes a difference if you're someone who doesn't like heights. I met mules on both trails, and it was definitely more comfortable making room for them on the Bright Angel Trail.

As I was hiking down the Bright Angel Trail, I couldn't keep my eyes off the scenery. The immense depth and length of the canyon and its careening contours hinted at the force of nature it had taken to create them. I kept snapping photos, with each new sight more incredible than the last. I wasn't sure how hard the steep hike out of the canyon would be, so the first day I just hiked to the mile-and-a-half rest house. I stopped for a snack and chatted with some of the other hikers resting there. As I was hiking back up the trail, I kept running into the same man over and over again. I would stop to sit on a rock and catch my breath from the steep climb, and we would exchange pleasantries as he hiked past me. A few minutes later, I would come upon him perched on a rock as he caught his breath.

"Where are you from?" I asked during one of our leapfrog exchanges.

"Minnesota," he replied.

"No kidding, I grew up in Minnesota." We chatted again on our next pass-by, and I learned that he had also just been to Zion and Bryce. *Small world. What are the odds?* He was attractive and seemed nice, and I didn't see a wedding ring. I briefly considered asking if he wanted to hike together or meet up later. Then I remembered my mistake with the Canadian and decided against it. *He's probably married.* When we reached the top of the canyon, I wrapped my cape of caution firmly around myself and said goodbye.

When I woke up the following morning, the muscles in my calves were complaining, but I was expecting that. I walked and fed Rylie before starting down the South Kaibab Trail. Soon after entering the canyon, I met Marie. She looked to be around my age, with short brown hair and a friendly face. She had a serious-looking backpack and hiking poles. We exchanged some pleasantries and introduced ourselves.

"Is this your first time in the canyon?" she asked.

"Yep, very first time. What about you?"

"No, I've been hiking to the bottom of this canyon every year on my birthday for the past twenty years."

"Happy birthday! What a great birthday present for yourself. Where are you from?"

"Portland. What about you?"

"San Francisco Bay Area."

"Where in the Bay Area? I lived in Walnut Creek until a few years ago, when I moved up to Portland."

"No kidding! I just sold my house in Concord, but I lived in Walnut Creek for ten years before moving to Concord."

We discovered that we'd lived in Walnut Creek at the same time, within a mile of each other. It really was a small world. We hiked together for quite some time and got to know each other better. Marie told me what it was like hiking to the bottom of the canyon and back up.

"There is one part of the trail that is really scary for me," Marie said. "It's a narrow rock ledge that has sheer drops on either side. I get vertigo, and it can get very windy in that spot.

Sometimes I have to get down on my hands and knees and crawl across."

"You get vertigo and you still hike the Grand Canyon every year?" I asked in amazement. I was impressed. This woman faced her fear head-on, year after year, and never gave in to it.

"Well, I'm not going to let fear stop me from doing what I want to do. If I do, fear wins."

"You're really gutsy," I replied. "I'm not sure I would have that much courage."

"You said you sold your house and quit your job to live in a motorhome when you had never driven a motorhome before," Marie said. "I'd say that's pretty gutsy."

Eventually, I had to turn around to make the slow climb back up the canyon. We bade each other farewell, but I thought about Marie with admiration for a long time afterward. She was an ordinary person, but she was very inspiring. I loved meeting people and learning their stories on the hiking trail.

My last evening at the Grand Canyon, it snowed. Since I grew up in the bitter cold and plentiful snow of Minnesota winters, I usually don't get too excited about snow. But even I had to admit that the large, lacy flakes looked beautiful as they danced their way to the ground. There were still some thin patches of it on the ground the next morning when I was leaving. After I hooked up the car and drove out of the campground, I felt sadness seeping in. I wasn't ready to leave the stunning beauty of this park. I regretted that I had not allowed more time here, but I had so many places to see, and the end of my one year of freedom was ticking closer.

CHAPTER 22

PLAN ADJUSTMENT

MAY-JUNE 2007

Independence is happiness.

—Susan B. Anthony

In early May, panic swept over me. I had been on the road for eight months, and I realized my year of traveling freedom would be done in four months. I felt like screaming, "No, I'm not done yet!" I was just getting the hang of managing my motorhome and adapting to life on the road. The old Heidi who had started this journey had been replaced by a new Heidi who was happy, confident, and free. I didn't want to go back to the rat race in four months. My bank balance was shrinking and I needed to start getting some money coming in, but I just couldn't go back to my old life and give up my newly found freedom. I needed to figure out a way to keep traveling.

During my journey I talked to many people who did work-camping. They found jobs they could do part-time or for short periods so they could hit the road when they weren't working. Some worked as campground hosts, others did sales, worked at festivals, or held many other kinds of temporary jobs. Not long after my panic, I received a phone call from Cindy.

"I got a work-camping job," she announced.

"No kidding, I was thinking about getting one myself. What are you going to do?"

"I got a part-time job at an RV park in Southern California. It's really nice, and I'm going to help out in the office. They pay me wages, plus I get to park the motorhome for free. I think they're looking for more workers. Do you want me to ask the manager if they're hiring more help?"

"Sure, why not?" Work-camping would help me to extend my travels a little longer. I thanked her for thinking of me, and she said she would call me when she found out more.

Cindy called me a few days later to tell me that they were still hiring. I applied and was hired to do whatever odd jobs were needed in the office or on the grounds. I left Arizona and traveled west on Interstate 10 into California, stopping to check out the Palm Springs area along the way.

The place I would be working was located in a remote spot in the hills near Temecula, between Los Angeles and San Diego. This was mostly desert country, and in May, it was already parched and sweltering. After I arrived at the RV park, I was greeted by Cindy's big grin. She showed me where to park my motorhome and car, and waited while I got settled in.

When I was done she said, "Come on, I'll show you around. It's a pretty big place, so we'll take the golf cart." The park had several golf carts that were used by the staff to do their chores and get around the park. She drove the different loops where the motorhomes were parked, pointing out the pretty ponds and fountains, the tennis courts, and a very inviting swimming pool. She pulled up to the clubhouse and parked the golf cart.

"Let's go inside so I can show you everything in here." We toured the fitness room, the book and movie library, and the main room where events were held. "They have rooms for playing cards and games, and for doing crafts, too."

"They have a lot of activities to offer here," I said. "It's really nice."

"The people are nice too. I think you'll like working here. It gets hot in the summer, though. Make sure you wear a hat if you work outside."

I started working soon after arriving at the campground. I spent some days in the office and others digging up weeds, feeding brush into the wood chipper, and doing other outside maintenance. Cindy was right, it was hot already, and summer hadn't arrived yet.

We spent many of our evenings together, and our friendship became even stronger. One of us was usually on call for any emergencies that might happen, so we had to stay put in the park.

Since I was only working three days a week, I had four days to explore the nearby areas. I loved the Central Coast area of California, including Cambria, a quaint town of about six thousand residents perched on the Pacific. I had friends living in the Central Coast area, so I visited as often as I could.

The drive from Temecula to Cambria was about three hundred miles, so I waited until my next long weekend and made the trip. I spent time with friends, poking around the art galleries and shops in Cambria and hiking in Montaña de Oro State Park, a gorgeous park with dramatic coastal views. We also attended the Strawberry Festival in Arroyo Grande.

As I drove back to the RV park, I realized how fortunate I was to enjoy my time of travel and still visit my family and friends fairly often. Gratitude had not been a familiar feeling for me before I started my life on the road. I'd been too wrapped up in my straitjacket of depression to feel gratitude back then, but I was overwhelmed with continuing waves of it now.

There was no Wi-Fi in the campground, except for a spotty connection at the top of a very steep hill about a half mile from where my motorhome was parked. This was before smartphones were common, and I didn't have one. I had to load my laptop into my car and drive to the top of the hill, then quickly answer my email and do any internet research I needed to do before my battery ran down. I checked my email once a day, at the most. I settled into my new routine and felt better that I had a little money coming in and could continue to travel beyond the year I had originally planned.

After weeks with no response from the Canadian, I was convinced that he was respecting my wishes and I would not hear from him again. Even though I knew what he had done to me was wrong and part of me was still angry with him for lying to me, part of me felt bereft. It was hard to let go of feeling like the center of someone's universe.

One day I made the drive up the hill and fired up my laptop, and there was his name in my email. It was surprising how easy it was to open his email this time; I didn't even hesitate.

My Beautiful Bella,

The beautiful things I told you were not lies. I meant every word. I didn't know that I could feel that way at my age. You brought me to life again. I understand why you don't want to get involved with me. But our time together was so special; I just can't let it go. I think about you all of the time. You make me so happy, and I get so excited when I see an email from you. I hope you will email me back just to let me know that you are okay.

The email went on to tell me how much our time together in Mexico had meant to him, how special I was, and that he cared for me very much. He told me again that he and his wife had been living separate lives for years. His letter was lengthy and filled with emotion and longing to see me. He asked if he could have my mailing address, to send me something in the mail.

Without thinking about it, I hit reply. My response was brief, but I let him know that I was okay, and busy with my work-camping job. I knew that I shouldn't, but I gave him my address. After the email was sent, I returned to the motorhome, feeling like I imagined a teenager must feel when they are caught shoplifting. Catching a glimpse of myself in the mirror, I whispered to my reflection, "What are you doing?"

A week later, I received a package in the mail. It contained an assortment of little trinkets a woman would enjoy, including scented massage lotion, a fancy nail file, gourmet food treats, and other assorted goodies. Tucked in with the gifts was another love letter. I was consumed with guilt as I read it. I didn't understand this stranger who was inhabiting my skin. *Why am I still in contact with this man?* I knew why. *Because he makes me feel good.* I was on a pleasure cruise, refusing to get off even though the boat was back at the dock. I brushed my guilt aside, telling myself it was a harmless diversion because I would never see him again.

About a month into my work-camping job, the vineyard next door started shooting off noise cannons to scare the birds and other critters away from the grapevines. The explosions were nonstop, and they terrified Rylie, who had always been afraid of thunder, fireworks, and any loud noise. It got so bad that he didn't want to go out of the motorhome to relieve himself. I would stop at the motorhome on my breaks from work to take him outside for a quick walk, but he started refusing to go outside. I had to carry him out and make him stay until he emptied his bladder. I felt awful for him. Cindy's dog was old and deaf, so fortunately, the noise didn't bother her.

I talked to the manager of the RV park and explained my problem. He talked to the vineyard owner to see if they would stop the noise but got nowhere. One day I arrived home from my break to find a mess of bloody diarrhea in the motorhome. Rylie never messed in the house or the motorhome, so I knew this was serious. I took him to the vet, who diagnosed ulcerative colitis, brought on by stress. I tried some of the remedies and medications recommended by the veterinarian, but they didn't seem to help much. We had to leave.

I told the manager of the RV park that I had to go, and we moved on. I was sad to say goodbye to Cindy and the other friends I'd made there, but it was well worth it. After a few days without the continual explosions, Rylie started returning to normal. We drove to the Bay Area to visit Cammie and ended up staying there for more than a month. I was a little nervous about how Rylie would handle the July Fourth celebrations, since there were often plenty of fireworks. Fortunately, none were nearby, and he got through the evening without becoming stressed and scared.

The holiday was the perfect time to think about independence and freedom. Specifically, my independence and freedom. For the past ten months, I had been free of debt for the first time since Cammie was born. Even better, I was free from what felt like the indentured servitude of a full-time, permanent job. Being debt-free and mostly jobless had increased my choices exponentially, and having a bouquet of choices really made me feel free. The frosting on the cake was having my little home on wheels, so I could travel wherever and whenever I pleased and stop and linger if I felt like it. This was total freedom, and I really had something to celebrate.

Our American culture raises us to be a society of consumers, believing we need to have the finest houses, cars, gadgets, and all of the other trimmings. But we don't realize how this unquenchable thirst for the latest and greatest things enslaves us and eliminates our choices. I discovered how freeing it was to give up my house and most of my possessions, and how much lighter I felt without them. I realized my traveling lifestyle was not for everyone, but it sure suited me at this particular time in my life. I knew that could change someday and that eventually I might want to stay put for a while, but not yet. I was really loving my life and feeling grateful for every day that I got to experience this adventure. I felt the most independent and free of my entire life, and boy did it feel good. Then I received another email.

CHAPTER 23

NOT DONE YET

JUNE 2007

Never revisit the past, that's dangerous.

—Robert Redford

I wondered if the Canadian knew how I turned to Jell-O every time I saw his name in my email, and how much I looked forward to reading his lengthy love letters. I didn't want him to know how much his emails were affecting me. I had never known a man who was as appreciative and attentive as he was. It was intoxicating. I wanted to be strong and cut off contact with him, but the truth was, every time he emailed me, I crumbled a bit more inside and my resolve to avoid him got weaker. I kept replaying our time together and how he made me feel, until his awful confession. I pushed that out of my mind. I couldn't seem to shake my neediness for romance. Feeling a confused hash of guilt and pleasure, I kept opening and responding to his emails.

I didn't understand my own behavior. I felt like I was betraying myself, and all of my principles, by staying in contact with this man. *Why am I behaving like a stupid schoolgirl with a crush? What is this hold he has over me? I am not as free and independent as I thought.* This last thought depressed me.

I consoled myself with the knowledge that it was only email, so it was harmless.

The email exchanges with the Canadian increased in frequency, and his emails became longer and filled with even more words of love and appreciation. I wrote responses in kind, telling him about the places I visited. We shared a love of travel and nature, and sometimes he seemed just as interested in my experiences as I was.

Meanwhile, I needed to get another part-time job so I could continue my journey. A month earlier, I'd learned about an interesting work-camping opportunity. One of the RV clubs published a monthly magazine for their members, and it was in one of these magazines that I read an article written by a salesman for an aerial photography company.

The article described how the author was able to work while he traveled around in his RV, selling aerial photographs. I thought this sounded like an intriguing idea, so I emailed him to ask him about the job. He wrote me back, explaining how it worked, and suggested that I call Jake, the sales manager in Washington, to find out more. He said he would pass along my name to Jake. I intended to email Jake and then got busy. A couple of weeks later, I received an email from Jake, who suggested that I call him. We ended up having a phone interview, and he encouraged me to give it a try.

The company sent me some aerial photos they had taken in Napa Valley, which was less than a couple of hours from where I was staying in the Bay Area. When I opened the package of photographs, I couldn't believe my luck. Almost all of the photos were of huge, beautiful homes surrounded by postcard-perfect vineyards and the gorgeous scenery of Napa Valley.

Napa Valley was the most famous wine-growing region in California. People came from all over the world to see the beautiful vineyards and sample the many wines offered in the tasting rooms. Mount Saint Helena sat at the north end of a valley adorned with lush grapevines everywhere you looked. I found a small campground in Napa and was lucky to get a campsite. I spent about a week driving around dozens of vineyards and going door-to-door, meeting the owners of these beautiful properties. Although I'm not the typical gregarious salesperson, I did very well selling the photos. Best of all, I had fun doing it. I enjoyed meeting and talking to people, and most were nice and friendly. I was paid strictly commissions, but when the sales were good, as they were in Napa, I could make decent commissions for part-time work. The photos were so pretty, they practically sold themselves.

Jake invited me to continue working for them, and I agreed. Since I planned to visit my family in Minnesota, Jake said they had some photos in Southern Minnesota that I could sell when I was done visiting with my family. I planned to go to Minnesota for about a month and prepared to hit the road. In my next email to the Canadian, I mentioned my plans.

"I'm on my way to see my family in Minnesota. We're going to the Boundary Waters Canoe Area together," I wrote. I told him how much I was looking forward to this family time, and that we had never been to that area before. "There's a black bear sanctuary not far from there that we plan to visit, too."

His response was sitting in my inbox the next day. Just the sight of his name caused me to flush with excitement. Now I fully understood the expression *guilty pleasure*.

"I can't believe the coincidence!" he wrote. "I am going to be in Thunder Bay visiting with friends around that time. That's only a few hours away from the Boundary Waters area. We are going to be so close—it must be fate. Please, Bella, could I come and see you there?"

My stomach turned somersaults as I stared at the question. I had not planned to see him again, so I'd felt that our email correspondence was pretty harmless. Seeing him in person would be a completely different ball game. I squirmed in my chair.

I knew that the right thing to do would be to say no. In the past, I'd never understood how women could get involved with married men. I thought they were fools who should know better. Granted, I didn't know the Canadian was married when I first met him, but I knew now. And yet, I was considering his request. Even though he'd lied to me about his marital status, I still wanted to believe what he told me was true, that he and his wife had lived separate lives for years. *That's basically divorced, isn't it?*

I'd spent my entire life trying to do the right thing, conducting myself with honesty and integrity in my relationships with other people and at work. I'd often denied my own wishes and desires to please and care for others, including my parents, my daughter, and the men in my life. This time, I wanted to be selfish and indulge myself in this romantic fantasy, even though my common sense told me it was just that—a fantasy.

I shoved aside my common sense and guilty conscience and typed, "Yes."

CHAPTER 24

BOUNDARY WATERS

JULY-AUGUST 2007

The older I get, the more I appreciate my rural childhood.

—Barbara Kingsolver

As the cornfields and prairie grasses of Southern Minnesota once again gave way to the lush woods and picturesque lakes of the northern half of the state, I found myself experiencing a familiar feeling of comfort and eager anticipation to see my family and the place where I grew up. My parents had lived in the same house since I was in the first grade, and seeing it always brought back a jumble of childhood memories.

My parents' house sat on one and a half acres, about half of which was heavily wooded. It had four small bedrooms, with dormer windows on the two upstairs bedrooms. Tall, nearly floor-to-ceiling windows covered three sides of the house, with a bay window off the dining and living room area, and everywhere you looked, there were trees. I have some vivid memories of playing in those woods with my sisters, my brother, and the neighbor kids. Sometimes we walked far back onto the property that bordered ours, which was owned by the Magnusson family. They had a farm with cows and a barn, and occasionally a litter of kittens. A couple of times we begged our parents to let us have one, but we were quickly denied. A thick rope hung from a huge oak tree on the edge of their property, with a large knot at the bottom. We took turns running off a small hill and hopping onto that knot, clinging to the rope as we flew back and forth like soaring birds.

Although there were bears and sometimes wolves in that part of the state, they did their best to avoid people, and we never ran into them as children. We also played in the road, but the travel was pretty light, and things were different back then. Parents didn't worry about kidnappings or keeping a constant eye on their children back in the 1960s and '70s, at least in rural Minnesota. We didn't lock our cars or our houses, except at night, when my mom locked the front door, for some strange reason. My parents both worked from the time I was eight, so we learned to be independent and self-sufficient, although the neighbor next door kept an eye on us.

Winters were hard in northern Minnesota, with temperatures often falling below zero and blizzards that dumped feet of snow overnight. One year the snowfall was so heavy that the snowbanks reached halfway up to the roof of the neighbor's garage. We climbed a ladder onto the roof and then jumped into the snowbanks below, laughing as they broke our fall. Another year an overnight blizzard deposited a snowdrift against our front door that was so tall, we had to jump out the window in order to catch the school bus in the morning. School closures due to snow were rare.

The worst part for our family was when the well ran out of water during the winter. That required frequent trips to the artesian well a mile up the road. There, water gushed nonstop out of a pipe and into a drain on the ground. We filled up water jugs so we had water for bathing, cooking, and drinking. I hated seeing all of that artesian water going to waste and couldn't understand why we never had enough water when it was so plentiful just a mile up the road. Then my dad explained that our house was built over rock, which meant we'd have to drill a long way through the rock to get to the water source below. It was very expensive to drill that deep.

Years later, after all of us kids were on our own and gone, my parents could finally afford to have a second well drilled. This well was much deeper than the original well and running out of water ceased to be a problem. Having to haul water in the bitter-cold winter taught me to appreciate what happens when you turn on a faucet, and what a luxury it is to take a long, hot shower during a cold winter.

Often the temperatures reached twenty degrees below zero, and with the wind chill factor, it could feel like the equivalent of two or three times that. We didn't have a garage back then, so as a teenage driver, I had to plug in the tank heater on my car on the nights when the temperatures got below zero so the car would start in the morning. Sometimes the snowplow would come by in the morning to clear the road, and the driveway would have to be shoveled out before we could go anywhere.

I loved to ice-skate, and there was an outdoor rink about a mile from my house. I would beg my dad to give me rides to and from the rink on the nights when he came home after work. One year I almost got frostbite on my cheek from staying out skating too long. It was a hard life growing up in the Minnesota winters where money and water were scarce, but we still found ways to play and have fun. The seeds were sown back then that grew into my hardworking, independent, and adventurous spirit.

Some of these memories danced through my mind as I drove up Lindahl Road and pulled into my parents' driveway. The house always looked smaller and older than I remembered it from childhood, but my parents had made improvements over the years, including building a garage.

As I pulled the motorhome into the driveway of my childhood home, my dad came out to greet me.

"Hello, hello!" he called out as he gave me a big bear hug.

"Hi, Dad. It's good to see you."

"I've been waiting all day for you to get here. I'll direct you so you can get the motorhome parked." He was taking charge of driving matters, as usual.

My mom came out with a big smile on her face and gave me a warm hug.

"I'm so glad you're here," she said, squeezing my hand.

"It's really good to be here, Mom."

With my dad directing me so that I didn't hit the well on one side or the garage on the other, I drove the motorhome onto the leveling blocks.

I'd originally planned to spend a couple of weeks at my parents' house, and then travel with my sister and brother-in-law to Boundary Waters. Now that I was going to meet up with the Canadian, I told my family I would be heading up earlier on my own so that I could spend a few days with him. I would meet up with them when they arrived.

The Boundary Waters Canoe Area was in the northeast corner of Minnesota. Strangely enough, during all of the years we had lived in Duluth, none of us had ever been there. We had driven up the north shore of Lake Superior all the way to Canada, but we never went to the Boundary Waters. This pristine wilderness area encompassed more than 1,700 miles and contained many lakes popular with fishing, canoeing, and kayaking enthusiasts. It was only a couple of hours away from where we lived. I had developed a greater appreciation for nature in my adult life, and I was eager to see it. It would be even more special to experience it with my family.

The Canadian and I worked out the details of when and where to meet. I found a campground where I could park the motorhome and made a reservation for the few days we planned to spend together. As I drove north, the thought of our spending more time together filled me with excited anticipation. I pushed my guilty conscience aside, instead choosing to remember the passion and romance we had shared in Baja. Although I felt nervous as I waited for him to arrive at the campground in the late afternoon, as soon as I saw him, the nervousness disappeared.

"Oh, Heidi," he said as he wrapped his arms around me. "I am so happy to see your beautiful smile. Thank you for agreeing to see me."

We got reacquainted over a bottle of his tasty homemade wine. He quickly put me at ease with his gentle, adoring ways and his quick wit. He seemed very concerned with making me feel comfortable, happy, and relaxed. We took a walk around the campground, holding hands, stopping a couple of times so he could take me in his arms and kiss me gently.

"Ever since Baja, I haven't been able to stop thinking about you," he said tenderly. "I'm so happy to spend time with you again."

"I'm happy to see you too," I replied, and I realized it was true. I was completely in the moment, with no thoughts of what would happen in the future. My only wish was for another few days as romantic and passionate as the ones we'd shared in Baja.

The many lakes of northern Minnesota produce a lot of wild rice, so it is a popular menu item there. I cooked some homemade chicken and wild rice soup that day, so we had a simple meal of soup, salad, and bread, and then the Canadian took Rylie for a walk while I cleaned up. When he returned, we relaxed over a glass of wine. Once again, he'd brought me thoughtful gifts from Canada, and I was feeling romanced and pampered. As the evening wound down, he led me into the bedroom, where the passion we had experienced in Baja was rekindled. Later, as he was holding me in his arms and stroking my hair, a song played on the radio about a couple running away together. The Canadian said, "I wish we could forget about the outside world and stay here forever."

Although the words were said tenderly, they came with a stinging reminder that he had another life—and a marriage—and I was a guilty party to an affair. I knew that a difficult conversation was coming, but I didn't want to think about it yet.

CHAPTER 25

BEARS

AUGUST 2007

The continued existence of wildlife and wilderness is
important to the quality of life of humans.

—Jim Fowler

T he next morning, the Canadian rose early.
"Sleep in," he whispered in my ear. "I'll take Rylie out for
a walk."

I luxuriated in my sloth while they walked. After shower-
ing and eating breakfast, we set out for the town of Orr, to visit
the Vince Shute Wildlife Sanctuary.

The sanctuary was a three-mile patch in the deep woods of
the northernmost part of Minnesota. Here the wild black bears
strolled in to eat nuts, berries, and other food provided for
them that was natural to their diet. The area was not fenced,
and there were no enclosures of any kind. There were wooden,
elevated viewing platforms where people could safely watch as
the bears came and went, eating, climbing trees, and sometimes
interacting with each other. Volunteers were available on the
platforms to educate visitors about these interesting animals.

The bears seemed to know they were safe in this area and
would not be harassed or shot by people, as they often were

outside of the sanctuary. Because of this, it was possible to see dozens of bears congregate as they drifted in and out for an easy meal. The number of bears that could be seen on any given day varied, affected by factors such as what other food in the forest was ready for eating.

Seeing animals in the wild always gives me such a thrill, and we hit the jackpot that day. We saw more than forty bears during our visit. There were huge boars, the males, lumbering below the platforms and taking over center stage. One bear was missing a paw, and I wondered if it had been caught in a trap. The feeding volunteers carefully walked well-worn paths between the different feeding spots to put out the food, and they often were very close to the bears. Neither the volunteers nor the bears seemed to mind, but I would have been nervous to be so close to these large and potentially dangerous animals. The serving dishes were tree stumps, logs, and hollowed-out pieces of wood. The volunteers carried large buckets of berries, nuts, fruits, and seeds that they dished out by the scoopful.

The sows, or female bears, sometimes came with cubs, which usually scampered up the trees right away. A volunteer explained that the sows sent their cubs up the trees to be safe while they were eating. Up in the tree branches, the cubs were often at eye level from the viewing platforms, which made for great photos.

My face was barely big enough for my grin as I took in all of those bears, my camera clicking nonstop. Although I had grown up in the woods of northern Minnesota, I had never seen bears so close, and certainly never in such huge numbers. I was happy that I got to experience this with the Canadian, and he was just as pleased as I was. We spent a lot of time just enjoying the bears. He kept me laughing and I felt confident and comfortable with him. He always seemed so concerned about pleasing me and making sure I was enjoying myself. I had never felt so cared for by a man, and it was very seductive.

I wondered what he got from our relationship, but after thinking about it, I thought I understood. Not only did I give him an escape from his unhappy marriage, but he got to visit me in different places. We could explore fresh landscapes and experiences together, and there was always something new and interesting.

The next morning, the Canadian woke me with a kiss. "I have a surprise for you today. It will probably take a couple of hours. Would that be okay?"

"Sure," I said. "What kind of surprise?"

"You'll just have to wait and see," he teased with a sly look. We got in the car and he drove to a municipal airport in Orr with a few small airplanes scattered around. He turned to me and said, "Would you like to go for a ride in one of those?" He pointed at the four-seater planes.

"I'd love to! I've never been in a plane that small." We saw a man who appeared to be in his late fifties walking toward us, and we went to meet Mike, our pilot.

"Heidi, you sit in front with Mike. You can see better that way. I'll sit behind you."

A few minutes later we were speeding down the runway, then immediately lifting into the air. As we climbed into the blue expanse above, I could see a carpet of green below us liberally sprinkled with sparkling pools of blue in this beautiful, lake-studded area. Suddenly, the Canadian reached over the seat for my hand, and I immediately knew why he'd arranged this. It was similar to the airplane scene in *Out of Africa*. The Canadian was a romantic, and this was his attempt to re-create that scene. I felt the tendrils of something soft and lovely winding around my heart.

On our last day together, we drove around the lushly wooded area and had dinner at a rustic-looking restaurant on a river. The food was simple but delicious, and we never ran out of conversation. As we were driving back to the motorhome, we got on the subject of regrets.

"I have very few regrets," I said. "I don't regret marrying my ex-husband, even though the marriage lasted such a short time, because I came out of it with a wonderful daughter. I do regret that I decided to wait a year after graduating from high school to go to college. If I had gone right after high school, instead of getting a full-time job, I probably would have gotten a degree in four years. I also would have had that immersive college experience that I missed, because I was working forty hours a week and going to school part-time."

"I have lots of regrets," the Canadian said. "My biggest regret is giving up a child for adoption. Before my wife and I were married, she got pregnant. We were young, and neither of us was ready to be a parent yet, so we decided to give the baby up for adoption. Later, when we decided we were ready to have kids, she couldn't get pregnant.

"We really regretted the decision to give up our son and wanted to get in touch with him. We were told that we could only contact him if he requested it. He never has. We didn't have any other children, and I am very sad about that."

I could tell that this memory still caused him pain, and the fact that he had chosen to share this story with me, when we had known each other such a short time, made my heart soften. He took my hand and added, "But I will never regret my time with you."

I smiled and squeezed his hand, but I couldn't help wondering if I would regret getting involved with him. The practical, commonsense part of me told me that I most certainly would. Nothing good could come of getting involved with a married man. This was a big mistake, and every time I thought of his wife, I was flooded with guilt. *What if he's lying and his wife still loves him? What if he still loves her? Why does this mistake feel so good?* I was confused by the conflicting thoughts in my head and the feelings in my heart. *Which should I believe, my heart or my head?* I was even more disturbed by my neediness for this inappropriate romance. *What happened to the strong, confident, and free woman I became?* I pushed the unwelcome thoughts away.

Back at the motorhome, the Canadian said, "I have another surprise for you." He took a gift bag out of his luggage and told me to open it. Inside the bag was a small velvet jewelry box. I opened the box and gasped. Inside was a simple but pretty diamond necklace.

"It's beautiful," I said. "But—"

"Please, Heidi," he interrupted. "I want you to have it, so when you wear it, you'll think of me."

"Thank you," I said, wrapping my arms around him and kissing him. "No one has ever given me such a nice gift." I put the necklace on, and it sparkled against my skin. I knew I was acting like a fool, and yet it didn't stop me from drinking in the romance like a desert nomad at a well.

The next morning, we took a last walk around the campground with Rylie, my hand in his. I didn't want to spoil the mood, but I knew I had to bring up the subject of his marriage. Fortunately, he beat me to it.

"I told you that my marriage has been over for a long time," he began. "That's true. We have been staying together out of convenience."

I was silent, but that sounded strange to me. By staying married, both of them were preventing themselves from finding happiness with someone else. Then a thought popped into my mind.

"Have you had any other affairs?" I asked.

The Canadian was silent for a moment, looking uncomfortable. "Yes, I have," he admitted.

I was crushed. I wanted to believe that this was the first time he had strayed—that these were special circumstances. "When?" I asked, my voice quiet.

"It was years ago. My wife found out about it, and she was really angry. I ended the affair and thought we could work on our marriage. We saw a counselor, but my wife never got over being angry. Sometimes she tolerates me, but we aren't close."

"Why do you stay?" I asked.

"We've been married for a very long time. I would like to leave, but it's going to take some time to get it all sorted out."

I let this sink in. I wanted to believe that he would leave his wife and we would somehow find a way to live happily ever after, but I knew better. The chances of that were pretty slim. I knew then that this would have to be the last time we saw each other. We had shared some lovely experiences, but I saw no future with this man. I felt myself pulling away emotionally as he packed his bag and put it into the trunk of his car.

"I'll send you an email to let you know I got back okay," he said. "Will you let me know when you get back?"

I nodded. "Sure."

"Thank you for letting me come and spend time with you." With that he kissed me and climbed into his car.

As I watched him drive off, I whispered, "Goodbye." I knew that I couldn't keep seeing this man, and that it would only end in heartbreak for me if I did. But the starving romantic in me had been completely hooked by this Romeo who knew all the right things to say and do to make me feel loved, appreciated, and sexy. After navigating the dry desert of my love life for so long, I had been willing to settle for a few sips of brackish water. I realized that romance and the passion wrapped inside it was my drug of choice, and I was addicted.

When I allowed my thoughts to creep down the dark corridor of this realization, I was filled with shame. My self-confidence sagged, and I wondered how I could do this to myself when I was so newly happy with my life. Clearly, I still had some work to do before I truly turned my life around.

I tried pushing the Canadian out of my mind to focus on my upcoming family get-together. I readied the motorhome and started driving to Ely, where I would be meeting up with my family. I felt the physical and emotional miles widen the distance between me and the Canadian, and a frigid wind cooled my heart.

My family rented a cute cabin on the water, and we relaxed and laughed over card games, saw the sights in the area, and just spent time together. We visited the International Wolf Center and the Dorothy Molter Museum, where we learned about these hardy residents of northern Minnesota. Dorothy was the last resident of the Boundary Waters Canoe Area Wilderness, and she had to be pretty tough to survive the harsh winters of northern Minnesota in such a remote location. She was yet another gutsy woman.

This family bonding time became even more meaningful to me years later, when my dad was diagnosed with Alzheimer's disease and trips like this became impossible. There was no sign of the disease on this trip, and we thoroughly enjoyed our time together.

The rest of the family wanted to visit the Vince Shute Wildlife Sanctuary, and I didn't mind seeing it again. We drove in two vehicles back to Orr. My dad rode with me, and he told me what his life was like when he was a child.

"My parents used to send me away to stay with relatives every summer," he said.

"Why did they do that?" I asked. I knew my dad's family was poor, but I had not known he spent summers away.

"I don't know. I guess so I wouldn't get into trouble."

I knew my dad had gotten into trouble when he was in his early teenage years and had to spend some time in a juvenile detention facility, but I didn't know he had been sent away repeatedly when he was younger.

"My old man was mean," my dad said. "He used to beat me when I got into trouble. The first time he ever hugged me and told me he loved me was when I left to go into the army. My mom never told me she loved me."

This was the first time I could remember my dad telling me some of the details of his childhood. He was gone a lot when I was growing up, either at work, involved with car racing, or at the bar with his buddies, so it was hard to connect with him. But on this drive my dad cracked open a window in the wall between us and let me peek inside. I felt compassion for what he had endured as a child and felt the seeds of understanding and forgiveness flourishing. The emotional distance between us began shrinking, and I was filled with gratitude.

When we arrived at the wildlife sanctuary, we found the rest of my family. There were far fewer bears than what I had seen with the Canadian. Instead of more than forty, there were a couple dozen, at the most. This was apparently because the bears were feasting on the hazelnut crop that had just ripened in the woods. Still, everyone enjoyed seeing the few bears that did make an appearance.

Too soon the family trip was over, and it was time for us to go our separate ways. I returned to my parents' house for a few days before hitting the road again. It seemed that each time I said goodbye to my parents, it got more difficult. I could see a little more gray hair and slower movements with every visit, and I never got to spend as much time with them as I would have liked. Something very tender had happened on this visit, and I couldn't hold back the tears as we said goodbye. I felt as though I was leaving behind something very precious that I might never get back.

CHAPTER 26

LONE WOLF

SEPTEMBER-DECEMBER 2007

When a person goes into a relationship emotionally needy,
they are not going to have discernment in choosing people.

—Jennifer O'Neill

I t was time to get to work. I still had some money saved from the sale of my house, but my bank balance had been steadily declining. I needed to sell some more aerial photos. After my successful sales in Napa, my manager was eager to get me working again to see if I could repeat the performance. The company had some old photos in the Twin Cities area, but the dated material really hurt sales. I moved on to Iowa, where sales were better. After that I visited Texas, Arizona, and Nevada, peddling photographs along the way. Except for Arizona, these were not top destinations on my bucket list, but I had to go to areas where the company had photos. Still, it allowed me to continue my life on wheels, seeing parts of the country I had never seen before.

In some areas sales were really slow, and in others they were pretty decent, but I wasn't making a lot of money. I could work part-time and work the days and hours I wanted to work, which was very important to me. I really liked having that flexibility and control over my own schedule. I wasn't ready to give up my hard-won freedom just yet, so the work suited me.

The company had a lot of photos in Pahrump, Nevada, which had a population then of less than forty thousand and was an hour away from Las Vegas. Although this high-desert town was not a destination I would normally have chosen, it was not far from Death Valley, which I had never seen. As I drove the back roads skirting Death Valley on my way to Pahrump, I saw craggy mountains striped like Easter eggs and knew I wanted to explore this national park. Pahrump would be a good base camp to do that.

There were enough aerial photos of Pahrump homes and businesses to keep me there for several months, but as I took a look around the town, I wondered if I wanted to stay that long. Pahrump didn't have much to offer. The main attractions seemed to be a run-down casino, a winery, a "gentlemen's club" on the corner of the main drag, and Sheri's Ranch, a brothel just outside of town. Prostitution was legal in Pahrump, so it was all out in the open. Other than the proximity to Death Valley and the Red Rock Canyon area near Las Vegas, the only thing that interested me was the winery, which I'd heard had a really good restaurant. Besides the brothel, which was apparently well-known, Pahrump's other claim to fame was that the movie *Mars Attacks* was filmed there, and the town was featured in the film.

The photo sales started out well, so I decided to stay and work for a while. There was an RV park that offered low-cost monthly rates. It was a no-frills park but had a nice community of travelers. It was here that I met Chantay, another gutsy woman traveling solo. Chantay was an artist who did illustrations for children's books, and since the recent sale of her home, she'd been traveling full-time in her motorhome.

"How do you find the space in your motorhome to do your artwork?" I asked.

"I just use the dining table, and store everything away in these bins when I'm done." She showed me the storage bins she had in the bench seats of the dining set. "I do watercolors, so the cleanup isn't a problem."

Chantay had a Class A motorhome, which are the big, bus-types, and it was much larger than mine. She even had a washer and dryer.

"Isn't this hard to drive?" I was picturing myself behind the wheel of that behemoth.

"You get used to it. I'm sure your motorhome took a while to get used to."

"I was nervous for about the first week," I agreed, remembering my cross-country maiden voyage. "And then any time I was driving up or down a steep mountain, in strong winds, in heavy traffic, on narrow roads, or in Los Angeles." I laughed, thinking of the many driving situations that made me nervous with the motorhome.

"Other than that, you're fine," Chantay said, grinning.

As the only single, full-time female travelers at the RV park, we found we had some seeds in common and our friendship bloomed. Chantay's border collie had passed away recently, and she enjoyed Rylie's company. She started joining us on our daily walks, and we sometimes ventured outside the RV park to explore. Chantay had been staying in Pahrump for months, so she showed me some of the sights around town.

The emails and phone calls with the Canadian had continued during the several months since I'd left Minnesota. Even though I was extremely bothered by his confession that this was not his first affair, I had not summoned up the courage to end the relationship. I was starting to get a bit lonely in Pahrump, and there wasn't much besides work to keep me occupied. It made me look forward to receiving his emails and phone calls even more. I believed him when he said he was in a loveless marriage and convinced myself that I was not doing any harm by continuing our relationship.

"Where are you now?" he asked not long after I arrived in Pahrump. I explained where Pahrump was. "I'd like to come and see you there. Would that be okay?"

I hesitated. As long as we were just emailing or talking on the phone, I could pretend that I wasn't doing anything wrong. But if he came to visit, that was different. I couldn't fool myself as easily. *Say no.*

"I don't think you'll like it here." I cowardly tried to avoid a direct answer. "There's nothing to do in Pahrump, and I'll be working. Vegas is an hour away. Besides, it's cold here." I tried to make the area sound as unappealing as possible.

"I don't mind. I could help you with your work. I just want to see you."

"Are you sure you won't be bored?" I was stalling.

"How could I be bored if I'm with you?"

"Well, okay." As soon as I said it, guilt flooded my veins and I regretted my decision. *I am such a wimp. Why didn't I say no? Where is my self-esteem?* I was settling for the scraps of a relationship with a man who was still married and whom I only saw every few months. We discussed the arrangements and I hung up the phone. I was disgusted with myself.

In the days leading up to the Canadian's arrival, my bipolar feelings fluctuated between wanting to cancel his trip and looking forward to his company. Pahrump was a windy, desolate landscape, and it brought out the loneliness in me that always seemed to be lurking in the shadows, waiting for a break in the action to insinuate itself. Although I was working, I wasn't thrilled with my surroundings, and there wasn't enough to do in Pahrump to distract me from my loneliness.

One day while working I was talking to a customer who lived in the desert scrub outside of town, where there was a lot of open space and the homes were few and far between.

"There's a wolf that lives out here," he told me, looking beyond me. "She showed up about a year ago, all skinny and limping. It looked like she got shot. I figured she couldn't feed herself, so I started leaving dog food out for her. It took a long time, but now she'll even get close enough for me to touch her. Here she comes now. I just didn't want you to freak out if she comes close."

I turned to look behind me and saw a white wolf with long legs advancing slowly, making a wide circle around me. Although there were wolves in northern Minnesota, I had never seen one in the wild. I felt a tingle of excitement at seeing this sad but beautiful creature, who was still limping.

I could see that she was skittish, and I didn't blame her for not trusting humans. After all, one had nearly killed her, in a really cruel way. By shooting her and not killing her, they had left her to starve to death. If this kind man had not fed her, she would have died a slow and painful death. Although she probably hated it, she needed what this man gave her. I couldn't help but wonder if she despised her neediness, as I despised mine. I needed the attention and romance the Canadian gave me, just as the wolf needed her bowl of dog food.

The Canadian planned to fly into Las Vegas and rent a car, so he arranged to meet me at my campsite in Pahrump. As I watched his rental car pull up next to my motorhome, I felt anxious. I wasn't sure if I wanted to see him, and he was staying for a week. He must have sensed my hesitation, because he seemed to take extra care to put me at ease with his charm. We talked about visiting Death Valley, hiking in Red Rock Canyon State Park, and spending some time in Las Vegas.

"I meant what I said about helping you," he said. "I don't want to interfere with your work, but if I can help you with it, I would like to do that."

He seemed sincere about wanting to help me, so I agreed to let him come to work with me the next day. He drove while I navigated and got the photos ready to show to the property owners.

"What is the best restaurant in town?" he asked as we were driving to the homes.

"The restaurant at the winery is supposed to be good, but I haven't been there yet."

"I think we should go there for dinner. Would you like that?"

"Sure, I'll see if we can get a reservation." I picked up the phone and made a reservation for that evening.

When we returned to the motorhome after work, we decided to take Rylie out for a walk. The Canadian took my hand in his while we walked. I always loved it when a guy held my hand while walking.

"Have you ever been to the bottom of the Grand Canyon?" he asked.

"No, I could only hike part of the way into the canyon, because I had Rylie waiting for me in the motorhome. Hiking to the bottom and back up requires an overnight stay for most people."

"Not if you fly out," he replied. "I found out you can take a helicopter down to the bottom, go for a boat ride, have lunch, and fly back out."

"That sounds pretty amazing."

"Would you like to do it?" he asked.

"That would be incredible." I was excited at the thought of flying into that beautiful canyon. When we got back to the motorhome, he got out his phone and made the reservation, checking with me first to see if it was okay to do it in a couple of days.

"They don't fly in bad weather," he said after he hung up. "Let's keep our fingers crossed for good weather."

The next day he drove the car and helped with framing the photos while I read the map, did the paperwork, and met with customers. He cheered when I made a sale and made me laugh when I didn't. I had to admit, work was a lot more fun with the Canadian in the car.

Later, as we were eating a delicious lobster bisque at the winery restaurant, he asked, "Do you need to work tomorrow, or can I persuade you to go to Death Valley for the day?"

"I can be persuaded to go to Death Valley," I said with a smile. "That's the nice thing about setting my own schedule."

We spent the next day exploring the park, which had a surprising variety of scenery. From the salty, cracked earth of Badwater Basin, 282 feet below sea level, to the polished stone walls squirreling through Marble Canyon, we enjoyed the diversity of Death Valley. But that wasn't the end of our sightseeing.

From there we went to Las Vegas, where the Canadian had reserved a hotel room for the duration of his stay in Nevada. I thought it strange at the time, but it wasn't until later that it occurred to me why he had reserved a hotel room in Las Vegas while he was with me in the motorhome in Pahrump. He'd probably had to tell his wife the name of his hotel while he was in Las Vegas, and if she checked, she would find out that he had a room reservation. For a middle-aged woman, I was naïve in many ways. He had suggested that we stay in his hotel room while we were in Vegas, but I told him Rylie wouldn't like staying in a strange hotel room, so we took the motorhome and parked in an RV park near the hotel.

The next day, we took Rylie for a hike in Red Rock Canyon, not far from Las Vegas. There was a lot of scrambling over huge boulders, which was a challenge for Rylie's short little legs. Without my asking, the Canadian gave him a boost now and then, and even carried him in some difficult spots. The view from the top allowed us to see for miles across the smoggy valley to the ragged mountain peaks on the other side. Next, we drove to Hoover Dam, to check out that great feat of engineering.

We planned to take the helicopter and boat ride in the Grand Canyon the following day, but when we woke up, it was windy and rainy. When we called to confirm our reservation, we were told they couldn't fly in the heavy winds, and all flights were canceled for the day. We were disappointed, but we made the best of it. We saw a couple of shows and explored the city instead. I also did some Christmas shopping, since the holiday was only a few weeks away.

After this whirlwind of activity, it was time for the Canadian to go back home. As we said our goodbyes, I thought once again that this would be the last time I saw him, but I didn't want to face that awful conversation.

CHAPTER 27

TWO RANCHES

JANUARY-AUGUST 2008

To be yourself in a world that is constantly trying to
make you something else is the greatest accomplishment.

—Ralph Waldo Emerson

After a fun week celebrating Christmas in the Bay Area with Cammie, I reluctantly returned to Pahrump for three more months of work. Two experiences in Pahrump challenged my ideas about confidence and where it comes from.

One day, some of the ladies at the RV park announced they were headed over to Shari's Ranch for lunch, and Chantay asked if I wanted to go along. Shari's Ranch was the brothel in town, and I was told they had a restaurant with pretty good food. I was curious to see what a brothel looked like, and so was Chantay.

When we pulled into the expansive parking lot of the enormous building, it wasn't what I had been expecting. It wasn't seedy looking, and it reminded me of an understated casino. As we were eating a tasty lunch, some of the "working girls" strolled around in their skimpy outfits. One of them came up to our table and asked if we would like a free tour of the place. Everyone in the group was curious, so we said yes.

The tour was led by a couple of the young women working there. According to our tour guides, this was the best place if you were in the business. They explained that women came from all over the world to be there because it paid very well and had good conditions. They were on duty at "the Ranch" for two weeks at a time, then were off for a while before they returned for two more weeks.

We were first shown the parade room, where the girls have to assemble when there is a customer, no matter the time of day or night. The customer selects the service he wants from the "menu" and the woman who will provide the service. One of the guides confessed that they were sometimes unhappy to get awakened for potential work in the middle of the night. Some women would do their best to look unappealing and grouchy, but that didn't always guarantee they wouldn't get picked. I was reminded of the indignity of having to go through the process of being picked by classmates for sports teams in gym class at school, but these women seemed to accept it as part of the work.

The girls were quite candid in answering our questions and said there were strict rules prohibiting drug use and that they were drug-tested frequently. I asked about their safety, but they assured me that any problems were extremely rare, and there was a panic button in each room, with a bouncer on alert nearby.

I couldn't help but wonder what these young women did when they got older. One of the women said she wanted to go to nursing school in the future because she liked helping people. She seemed friendly, and since it was a legal business there, they were very open and matter-of-fact about what they did. It was a very educational tour, and certainly not something you run into every day. As they described their profession, I was struck by the fact that these women seemed very self-confident and in control. I wondered if that impression was accurate, or if they had some hidden insecurities that kept them in this profession.

The other interesting diversion was when I sold an aerial photo to a woman who owned a horse ranch. I saw that she had a Brahma bull and asked if she would mind if I took a photo of it. I had never seen a Brahma bull before, and he looked quite unusual, with a hump on his back like a camel's. She agreed, and even brought out a treat for the bull, named Benny, so that he would come over to the fence for the photo. I learned that in spite of his scary size and horns, Benny was afraid of the horses, and he retreated when they came over to investigate. Life and nature were full of surprises. Here was this huge animal that vastly outweighed the horses and was even armed with dangerous horns, yet he had a confidence problem. I learned that lack of confidence isn't just a human condition. It's everywhere.

I was learning so much during my travels and meeting some very nice people. This adventure was feeding my curiosity and my thirst for new experiences, even in Pahrump, where I didn't think I would find anything of interest to me.

March rolled around, and after such a long time in this town with not much to offer, I was chomping at the bit to put Pahrump in my rearview mirror. It was like living in a sepia photograph, with nothing but shades of brown—and lots of wind. I was feeling light-hearted when I finally drove out of town. I didn't realize how starved for color I was until I reached the green vegetable fields near Bakersfield, California. Suddenly, my world was transformed from a sepia photograph to living color.

I spent spring and part of summer camped in Morro Bay on California's Central Coast, peddling aerial photos in the inland areas. This was my favorite part of California, so I was really happy to spend a few months there enjoying the beautiful ocean views and small towns.

From there, I moved on to Portland for my next aerial photo sales work. I loved Portland too, and enjoyed exploring the Columbia River Gorge not far from the city. I received an email from Frankie, who asked if I would like to get together with her and Stan while I was in the area. This was the couple that I had enjoyed so much while I was in Baja, and I jumped at the chance to see them. They had a house in a Portland suburb, where they lived when they were not traveling in their motorhome, and I agreed to meet them there.

"It's so good to see you!" I gave them each a hug and realized how much I'd missed this nice couple and the time we'd spent on El Coyote Beach together.

They gave me a tour of their home, and we took a drive to a restaurant at an old logging camp to have lunch. We talked about how much fun we'd had on the beach and where we had traveled since then.

"We're going to go to a motorhome get-together up here in September at Fort Stevens State Park on the coast," Frankie said. "You should think about going. It's a fun group."

"That does sound like fun," I said. "I'll think about it and let you know."

As we said goodbye, we promised to meet up again soon, if not at the Fort Stevens get-together, then somewhere during our travels.

There was another couple from my company selling aerial photos nearby, so we met up one night for dinner to get to know each other. Pat and Jim told me about some of the areas they had worked and the places where the sales had been good, as well as the places to avoid. It helped me feel better to learn that some of my coworkers had had similar experiences with poor sales.

After giving it some thought, I decided to attend the motorhome get-together at Fort Stevens State Park. I emailed

Frankie to let her know I would be joining them next month and made my reservation with the group.

The emails and phone calls with the Canadian continued during this time, but one call in particular caught my attention. "I have some news," he said after I said hello. "I left my wife."

CHAPTER 28

OUT OF THE SHADOWS

AUGUST 2008

I have come to believe that there are infinite passageways out of the shadows, infinite vehicles to transport us into the light.

—Martha Beck

"What do you mean?" I was stunned and wasn't sure that I understood what the Canadian just told me.

"I moved out. We're getting a divorce."

Although the Canadian had told me that he and his wife didn't get along and lived separate lives, he'd never said he was planning to move out any time soon. I was unprepared for this announcement.

"Wow. I didn't know you were planning to do that. Did you file for divorce?" I asked.

"She did. We thought it would be better that way."

"Where are you living?" I asked.

He explained that he was temporarily staying at a friend's place, but that he would be moving into his own place in a few weeks.

"After I get settled in, I would like it if you would come and visit me here. Would you like to do that?"

"Yes, I would." My head was spinning with this unexpected news.

"In the meantime, you're not that far away. Can I come and visit you in Portland?"

I agreed that he could, and we made plans for a short visit in the coming weeks. After we hung up, I thought about this news. Although I was happy that he was getting the divorce and I would no longer have a relationship with a married man, I remained cautious. After all, our relationship had started on a lie. *Can I trust him?*

During his visit a few weeks later, we took Rylie on the Angel's Rest hike in the Columbia River Gorge. We panted and sweated our way up the steep sides of the gorge, but it was well worth it. The view of the river and gorge from the top was spectacular.

Another day, we attended a fun outdoor concert not far from where I was staying. We also took a drive to Mount Saint Helens to view the effects of the 1980 volcano eruption. The top of the volcano was wearing a turban of clouds and fog, but we could still see remnants of the devastation for miles. I had visited in the early 1990s with my parents, and nature had recovered quite a bit since. Back then, the corpses of thousands of trees had been scattered across a barren landscape like a giant box of toothpicks dropped on a gray carpet. Now young trees and fluffy foliage provided a soothing green bandage, with the decaying trees peeking through here and there, hinting at the healing that had taken place. I wondered if trust could be regenerated in a relationship like the greenery in nature.

When we returned to the RV park, the Canadian looked at the rusty old bike that I had been traveling around with and raised his eyebrows. I had been given this bike by someone who was getting rid of it, and my only cost had been to buy a new seat. When I was traveling, it was in a bike rack on the back of the car, so it had seen quite a bit of weather, and it showed.

"Would you like a new bike?" he asked.

"Well, sure, but I hate to spend money on a new bike when it'll be exposed to the rain and the rocks that are spit up from the road."

"Come on, let's go to the bike shop and just see what they have," he suggested. We went to a bike shop not far away, and the Canadian talked to the salesman about the type of riding I did.

"You might enjoy a hybrid," the salesman said. "They're a cross between a road bike and a mountain bike and are better for the type of trails that you usually ride."

"Give it a try," the Canadian suggested. "Just see if you like it. You don't have to buy it." He was very persuasive.

I gave the bike a test ride and had to admit that it was really nice, and a much better ride than what I had been using. Still, I hesitated at the $500 price tag.

"I would like to buy it for you," the Canadian said. "Then we can go bike riding together."

"No, it's too much," I protested. I was unaccustomed to men buying me expensive gifts, and he had already been too generous with the gifts during our other visits. It made me uncomfortable. We finally agreed to split the cost.

Soon it was time for the Canadian to make the trip back home. We discussed my upcoming visit to Canada, which was planned for the fall. I was excited—I could go visit him and see where he lived. Finally, our relationship was coming out of the shadows.

CHAPTER 29

UNEXPECTED VISITOR

SEPTEMBER 2008

I always try to take the unexpected things and make them work for me.

—Paul Watson

"I'm going to Fort Stevens State Park for a Lazy Daze group camping weekend," I told the Canadian during one of our phone calls.

"When are you going, and what will you do while you're there?"

I told him when I was going and the activities that were available there. "Frankie and Stan, the couple I spent time with in Baja, are going, too."

"It sounds like a fun weekend."

A few weeks later, I drove the motorhome to Fort Stevens State Park, arriving on a Friday afternoon. I was getting settled into my campsite when my phone rang. It was the Canadian.

"I have a surprise," he said.

"Really? What is it?"

"I'm here."

"Where? What do you mean?" I was confused.

"I'm here at Fort Stevens State Park."

"Really?" I paused, stalling for time. I was not pleased, but I didn't want to be rude. I had not invited him to come, and I had been looking forward to spending time with Frankie and Stan, and the rest of the motorhome gang. With the Canadian there, I would feel obligated to focus on him and make sure he felt comfortable with the group. I also thought it was presumptuous of him to think he could just show up uninvited when I had plans with friends. He certainly wouldn't have wanted me to surprise him that way. *What does it mean that I'm not happy about his surprise visit?* Another fissure had appeared on the surface of our relationship, but I didn't want to see it.

I swallowed my displeasure, summoned up some enthusiasm, and said, "Great!" I gave him directions to find my motorhome. I was in the middle of making a complicated appetizer to bring to the happy hour potluck that evening. I found myself getting stressed and crabby as I struggled with the new recipe and he hovered nearby in the small space. I was still feeling a bit annoyed at the way he had just shown up and assumed I would be available. I pushed my annoyance aside, and we went to join the happy hour.

The Canadian turned on his usual charm and fit right in with the rest of the group, making people laugh. During the weekend, we went for a walk around the pretty, tree-rimmed lake and to the beach, to see the shipwreck remains lurking in the spooky fog. We also went for a bike ride with Frankie and Stan to check out the fort. The Canadian had brought his bike and I got to enjoy my new bike. I remembered his generosity and felt guilty for being annoyed with him. At one of the stops during the ride, the Canadian braked suddenly and went headfirst over his handlebars, ending up on the ground.

Once we saw he was not hurt, Frankie called out, "Nice dismount!"

The Canadian laughed and said, "That's what I get for showing off."

Later, when he and Stan had wandered off and I was alone with Frankie she said, "I like him. He seems like a nice guy."

"He is a nice guy," I agreed. I didn't tell her about the lie that started our relationship.

The Canadian and I finished off the weekend with a drive to Astoria, where we had lunch. Then it was time for him to head back north, but we knew we would see each other in a few weeks, when I went to visit him in Canada.

I was glad that I had been able to put my annoyance aside and enjoy the weekend with him, although I didn't spend as much time with Frankie, Stan, and the rest of the group as I would have if he wasn't there. I was still unsure what would happen with his marriage. I figured there was a chance they could reconcile. Before now, I had always considered our relationship temporary. I'd figured he would stay in his marriage, and I would eventually break it off.

Now that it appeared he was really getting a divorce, I was starting to look at him and our relationship differently. The question was, did I like what I saw? We had fun together and he certainly knew how to bring the romance—more than I could have imagined. But was he the kind of man I wanted to have a long-term relationship with? Knowing he had lied to me about being divorced and that he'd had more than one affair, I wasn't sure I could trust him. *Will he lie to me again?*

CHAPTER 30

A TASTE OF CANADA

SEPTEMBER 2008

To love oneself is the beginning of a lifelong romance.

—Oscar Wilde

I pushed my nagging doubts about trust out of my mind and made plans for my trip to Canada. The Canadian had moved into a cottage, so a few weeks later, I left the motorhome in Portland and drove up to the Vancouver area in my car.

From the moment we arrived, the Canadian went out of his way to make both me and Rylie feel welcome and comfortable. When I knocked at his door he opened it and immediately gathered me in his arms. "I'm so happy you're here," he said, smiling. He greeted Rylie and patted him on the head. "I thought I would make pasta for dinner. Is that okay?"

"That sounds wonderful," I said, impressed that he was cooking a meal for us. "What can I do to help?"

"Nothing. Just sit there with a glass of wine and talk to me while I cook."

"With pleasure!" I smiled. I fed Rylie his dinner, then sat down to watch the Canadian cook while I sipped my wine.

We enjoyed the tasty meal and then talked as we finished our wine.

"I need to walk Rylie. Is there a good place nearby for us to go?" I asked.

"I'll come and show you."

I held his hand as we walked Rylie, who was happily exploring the intoxicating new smells of Canada.

When we returned to the cottage, the Canadian said, "I thought you might be tired from the long drive. I have some bath salts. Would you like to relax in the tub?" He led me to the freshly scrubbed bathroom, and I could see the tub was lined with candles.

"Wow," I said, impressed. "You really know the way to a woman's heart." It had been ages since I'd had a bubble bath. The motorhome had only a tiny shower, and after the long drive, I was ready to relax in a bubble bath.

The Canadian lit the candles and ran the bathwater. Then he said, "I'm going to open another bottle of wine." He headed to the kitchen while I slipped into the tub. He returned a few minutes later with a glass of wine for each of us. He handed me a glass and said, "I have something else for you." He disappeared to the kitchen and before he came back into the bathroom he said, "Close your eyes."

I closed my eyes.

"Now smell, but don't open your eyes."

I inhaled. "Chocolate," I sighed.

"Yes, and I think you're going to like it," he said as he put one into my mouth.

"Mmmmm, it's so good," I said, savoring the tasty treat. "You thought of everything. I feel so pampered and cared for. Thank you for this." I reached toward him and gave him a kiss.

While I luxuriated in my bath, he sat on the floor of the bathroom near the tub and fed me chocolates and talked quietly with me. I had thought the bath might just be a ploy to get me naked, but he made no attempt to put the moves on me. Instead, he only seemed concerned with making me feel comfortable and relaxed. He was not in a rush. It was the most romantic thing a man had ever done for me, and it was extremely seductive.

Over the next several days, the Canadian made sure that I got to see a sampling of the sights in the area. We drove the winding road up to Whistler, where he pointed out the highway-widening and other construction projects they were doing to gear up for the 2010 Winter Olympics. We stopped along the way at a river where he said bald eagles liked to congregate to fish. Unfortunately, it was still too early in the season for the eagles, and we didn't see any. Whistler, a popular skiing destination, was a beautiful mountain village. Tourists were already buying Olympic souvenirs, and the Olympics were still more than a year away. From the number of bicyclists we saw, it appeared it was also a popular place for mountain biking in the warmer months.

Another day we went to Steveston, a pretty coastal town near Vancouver. We checked out the catch of the day on the fishing boats and had a tasty lunch of fresh fish on the wharf. In Vancouver we visited the enormous Stanley Park and walked the beautiful trails winding near the water. The trees were showing their fall wardrobe, and it was stunning. The Canadian was an excellent host and tour guide, and he made sure that I was comfortable and happy, and that I got to enjoy as much of the area as I could during my short visit. Those few days flew by, and since I had to get to my next work location, it was time to say goodbye.

"What are your plans?" the Canadian asked.

"I'll be in Yuma until just before Christmas, and then I'll head to the Bay Area to spend the holidays with Cammie. After that I head to Phoenix."

"I'd like to come and celebrate your birthday in Phoenix. Would that be okay?"

"That would be wonderful." I smiled. Since my birthday is in early January, I was able to say goodbye without too much sadness, because I knew we would see each other in a couple of months. Now that he had left his wife, I didn't have mixed feelings about his coming, like I had during his other visits. Finally, I could look forward to his visit without guilt.

CHAPTER 31

THE BREWING STORM

OCTOBER 2008-JANUARY 2009

Character is formed in the stormy billows of the world.

—Johann Wolfgang von Goethe

I stopped for a visit with Cammie on my way to Yuma, and she seemed happy and busy with friends. I no longer felt like the mother hen abandoning her chick. I took care of some routine medical and dental appointments while I was there and then hit the road again, stopping along the way for a quick visit with Lucy and Annie. I had not seen Lucy since our Baja trip, and it had been two years since I had seen Annie. I was so happy to be with these wonderful traveling friends and grateful that we were still in touch, even if it wasn't very often.

Shortly after I arrived in Yuma, I got an email from Frankie. "Stan and I are camped just outside of Yuma. Do you want to get together?"

"Definitely!" I wrote back. We met for dinner, and they said they were staying for a few days while they got some dental work done across the Mexican border in Los Algodones.

"We're going to hike up to Pilot Knob tomorrow. You can see for miles up there. Do you want to join us?"

"Sounds great. Count me in." I'd had so much fun with them on El Coyote Beach and at Fort Stevens, I knew it would be a good time. They were always ready with a laugh, a good story, or help, if you needed it.

We arranged a time for the following day, and I drove out to meet them. When we got to the top of Pilot Knob, we stopped to take in the view. The brown desert carpet stretched for miles, and we could see the Mexican town of Los Algodones off in the distance.

"We're going to Los Algodones tomorrow," Frankie said. "You're welcome to join us."

"I'd love to." I had never been there, so I decided on the spot to take another day off to see it. It would be much more fun with Frankie and Stan than if I went on my own. Also, Frankie and Stan were leaving the next day to head to Baja, so I wanted to spend as much time with them as I could.

We parked the car on the US side and walked across the border. We poked around in some shops, and I bought a few pieces of Mexican pottery. We loitered to watch some of the artisans making their creations in the streets and then stopped for shrimp tacos at a popular taco stand. It brought back fond memories of my time of freedom and fun on the Baja Peninsula. Frankie and Stan pointed out the dentist office where they had their work done. The waiting room was filled with Americans there to get inexpensive dental work.

As we walked back over the border and prepared to say goodbye, Frankie said, "You should come to El Coyote Beach this winter."

"Oh, I would love to, but I can't. I really need to make some money for a while. That year I took off from work set me back financially. I need to save for retirement, so I can travel all of the time, like you two." This couple knew how to do retirement the way it should be done. They'd retired young, they spent every winter on El Coyote Beach, and they explored the country in their motorhome, hiking, kayaking, boating, and making friends everywhere they went. I was sorry I couldn't join them on the beach.

Sales were good in Yuma. Although it was still pretty hot when I arrived, the weather soon simmered down and became very pleasant. I was enjoying my stay, and my nightly phone conversations with the Canadian had become a habit.

"I made my flight reservations," he announced on the phone one night. We had already agreed on the dates, and his visit was only a few weeks away. "I asked my nephew to stay here and take care of things while I'm gone."

"Great! I'm really looking forward to your visit," I responded.

"Me too. I'm going to be busy for the next few weeks, though. I joined a softball team, so we'll be practicing and having games every week, plus I need to do some extra work so I can take time off for the trip. I might not be available to talk as often in the evenings."

"I didn't realize softball teams played this late in the season."

"It's just a casual league through work. We're not on the usual schedule."

"Sounds fun. It's okay if we don't talk as often, we'll be seeing each other soon. I'm going to be working a lot anyway, so that I can take some time off when you come to Phoenix."

The next morning as I headed out early to work, I saw clouds sidling together off in the distance. It almost looked like fog. A storm was brewing. I hurried to get some sales as quickly as I could, fearing that rain would chase me home early. But instead of rain clouds, a dust storm blew in.

I had never experienced a dust storm before, and the plentiful desert sands of Yuma conjured up great dust devils. Dirt swirled into funnel clouds like mini tornados, appearing all of a sudden out of nowhere. No one would want to be out in that cyclone of soil. Even without getting caught in a dust devil, my eyes and throat were filled with grit. Fearing it would get on the aerial photos I was selling, I decided to call it a day.

Although the dust storm cleared up the next day, the Green Monster had its own storm brewing. The water heater wouldn't turn on. I went outside and opened the water heater compartment. I checked the connections, but I couldn't see anything that looked amiss, so I called the local RV repair shop.

"Sometimes the circuit boards go bad. You can bring it in and we can test it," said the helpful service technician.

I removed the circuit board and brought it into the shop, but it tested fine.

"Do you want to make an appointment to bring the motorhome in?" the tech asked.

"Do you make house calls?" I asked. "I really don't want to move the motorhome just yet."

"No, sorry."

"That's okay. Thanks for your help." When I got back to the motorhome, I called Bruce, an RV repairman who had recently done some work on my refrigerator. There had been a recall, and a part had to be installed to prevent the refrigerator from overheating. I was pleased with his work, so I called to see if he could fix my water heater.

"I can come out tomorrow morning," he said. After a brief examination of the water heater the next morning, he identified the problem. "You have a bad thermo fuse. It probably went bad because of all of the dust here lately."

He had to use a special tool to install the part, so that made me feel better about my helplessness. As much as I wanted to be independent and solve problems myself, this was beyond my skill and tool set.

The Green Monster's shenanigans were not done. A short time later I was washing my hands in the bathroom sink and turned off the faucet. The water kept running. I tried several times, but the water would not turn off. The beast wanted a new bathroom faucet, too. I turned off the water supply outside the motorhome and called Bruce. I knew nothing about plumbing.

"How experienced are you with plumbing?" I asked.

"I do plumbing all the time," he responded. He came out and got to work. The bathroom was so tiny, he practically had to stand on his head to do the work. He also had to run to the hardware store for extra parts, but finally, he was done. A shiny new faucet gleamed on top of the sink, and it worked. He collected my check, packed up his tools, and left.

"There," I said to the Green Monster. "Are you happy now?" I was spending more on motorhome repairs than I had planned on, but it was still costing a lot less to live than when I was paying a mortgage, and I was enjoying working in short sleeves and sandals.

By mid-December, my work was done in Yuma. It was time to hit the road again. I stopped along the way for a quick visit with Cindy in Temecula, then headed to Pismo Beach for a visit with friends in the area. Cammie came down for the weekend, which made it even more fun. We went to Monarch Grove, a stand of eucalyptus trees near Pismo Beach where the monarch butterflies liked to spend the winter. The tree branches wore orange and black sleeves of butterflies, most of which appeared to be napping. It was amazing to see so many of them concentrated in one spot.

We also visited the elephant seal colony near Cambria and were lucky to see the first seal pup born that season, shortly after it was born. We huddled in the cold wind for a while watching to see if it would figure out how to nurse, but it was still fumbling around the body of its mother when the frigid air finally drove us back to our car. Nature operates on its own schedule, and we all lose our way sometime during our lives. I certainly had.

I returned to the Bay Area to spend the holidays with Cammie. California felt cold, which was surprising, considering I grew up in Minnesota. It doesn't take long to get spoiled by warm weather. Despite the cold, I was so happy to spend time with Cammie. I wasn't homesick this time, as I was my first Christmas in the Bay Area. I loved not having a rigid work schedule and being able to decide when and how much I wanted to work, and when I wanted to spend time with family or friends. Freedom was a very tasty brew, and I liked it. I was enjoying having an unconventional lifestyle. Of course, there were consequences, such as the small checks on payday, but considering I wasn't working forty hours a week, it wasn't bad.

By early January I was heading to Phoenix. I felt very fortunate to be spending the winter in Arizona. But as much as I enjoyed the balmy weather, I wasn't enjoying the people. They just weren't as friendly as they were in Yuma, or many of the other areas where I sold aerial photos. I worked for about a week logging pitiful sales, and then it was time for a break. The Canadian was coming to visit, and he had a birthday surprise for me.

CHAPTER 32

FLYING HIGH

JANUARY 2009

Whenever I dream about flying, it's the best feeling in the world.

—Kate Mara

"Would you like to go for a balloon ride on your birthday?" the Canadian asked soon after he arrived.

"I would love to!" A hot-air balloon ride was still on my bucket list. The Canadian made the arrangements, and before dawn on the morning of my birthday, we arrived at the launch site. We watched as they inflated the balloon, and then we climbed into the basket with the other passengers. Although the desert scenery was not as beautiful as a ride in a river valley or Napa Valley might have been, I really enjoyed the experience. I thought I might be a bit nervous, but it was incredibly peaceful floating soundlessly through the air, except for the occasional gasp of the propane burner. We were warned that the landing could sometimes be a bit bumpy so we prepared for some roughness, but our pilot expertly glided down and the basket gently kissed the ground. It couldn't have been a smoother landing. The crew had traveled ahead of us to the landing spot, where they set up tables for our champagne breakfast.

They even had a birthday pastry for me, and everyone sang the birthday song.

The Canadian was not done spoiling me. He took me out for a fancy steak dinner later that evening, and also presented me with a beautiful silver and gold bracelet. I saw the great effort and expense the Canadian went to, and I was swimming in love and appreciation.

During this visit the Canadian and I didn't talk about the future or what would happen when his divorce was final. He was focused on getting through the messy divorce proceedings, and I didn't know how long I would be traveling or what I would do when I stopped. From the day we'd met, I'd tried to be in the moment and enjoy our time together, without fretting about the future.

This visit was shorter than the others—only four days—so it was soon time for him to return north. "Thank you for the wonderful birthday celebration," I said, wrapping my arms around him and giving him a lengthy kiss. "It was incredible."

"You deserve to be celebrated," he responded. "Maybe I can come and see you again in a few months. Would you like that?"

"Yes, I would." I smiled. I knew that a few months would pass quickly. My parents were arriving for a two-week stay, plus Cammie and her boyfriend had planned a short visit. Between work and spending time with family, I would be very busy.

"Before I leave, I want to stop at the bike shop."

"What do you need at the bike shop?" I asked.

"I just want to see if they have something in stock." He pulled into a bicycle shop not far from where the motorhome was parked. We walked in and he brought me straight to where the bike accessories were.

"You still don't have a basket for the bracket on the back of your bike. Look around and let me know if you see one you like. I'd like to get one for you."

"No, you've done too much for me already. I can take care of that. But I'll see what they have." I wandered through the baskets and other containers of various sorts but didn't see what I wanted. "Can you order any others?" I asked the young man working behind the counter.

"Yes, let me show you what we can order in the catalog." We bent over the catalog together as he thumbed through the pages until he found the baskets. "We can order anything on these pages."

I looked through the pages. "I like this one." I pointed to a basket. "Can you order it?"

"Let me check." The clerk punched some numbers into the computer. "Sorry, this one is out of stock. Is there another one you like?"

I looked at the catalog some more, then shook my head. "No, none of the others is quite right. I'll check back later to see if it's in stock."

"You don't see anything else you like?" The Canadian walked up just then, after wandering around the store while we looked at the catalog.

"No, I really like this one in the catalog. I think I'll wait to see if they get it in stock." I thanked the store clerk for his help and we left. We drove back to the motorhome, and the Canadian put a few last items in his travel bag and zipped it shut.

"I saw that one of the tires on your bike is missing a tire stem cap," he said, taking something from his pocket and reaching for my hand. He placed a tire stem cap in my palm.

I looked at the cap, confusion furrowing my brow. "But when did you get this? You didn't buy anything at the bike shop."

"I took it off one of the bikes," he said with a little laugh.

I was appalled. "You stole this?"

"It's such a little thing, it's not a big deal."

I looked at him. The sun was streaming in the window, lighting up his face. I noticed his half-lidded eyes and thin lips. Suddenly, he looked unattractive, reptilian. My romance-colored glasses had fallen off, and I was starting to see clearly. I couldn't understand why he would spend lavish amounts of money on jewelry and entertainment, and then steal something that cost so little. It didn't make sense to me.

"Well, it's a big deal to me. I can buy one." I gave the cap back to him.

I saw a frown flash across his face, but he quickly apologized. "I better go if I'm going to catch my plane."

We gave each other a quick hug and kiss goodbye, but as I watched him drive off, I felt uneasy. *Do I really know this man?*

CHAPTER 33

SNAKES AND SURPRISES

FEBRUARY-APRIL 2009

Trust is the glue of life . . . It's the foundational principle that holds all relationships.

—Stephen Covey

I shoved aside my doubts about the Canadian to enjoy another visit from family. My parents, Cammie, and her boyfriend came to Phoenix and we enjoyed some of the sights of the area, including walking among the fifteen hundred petroglyphs at the Deer Valley Rock Art Center. Since I'd started traveling, I was seeing my family more frequently than when I worked in California and Cammie was at college in Colorado, which boosted my love of the lifestyle even more.

I finished up my work in Phoenix and rolled up the highway to Tucson. This city appealed to me much more than Phoenix. For one thing, the scenery was more interesting. Tucson sat along the banks of the Santa Cruz River and was cuddled by four mountain ranges. The Santa Catalinas lay to the north, the Rincons to the east, the Santa Ritas to the south, and the Tucsons to the west. The flat, brown carpet of Phoenix had been replaced with saguaro cactus soldiers dotting the high-desert valley and rugged mountains, and it looked green from a distance.

I worked in the rural areas on the outskirts of town, where the homes sat on large parcels of property. As I talked with my customers, I quickly learned that rattlesnakes were plentiful in this area. I heard stories of dogs and cats that had been bitten by rattlers, and how the snakes often made unwelcome appearances in yards. I had encountered rattlesnakes from a safe distance a few times while hiking in California, so I knew to steer clear of them.

One day I was hurrying up the curved, stepped walkway of a home with an aerial photo. I froze in my tracks when I suddenly realized that I was two feet away from a snake that was stretched out and sunning itself against a two-foot-high stucco wall on the right side of the walkway. As my eyes quickly darted to the tail of the snake to see if it had the telltale rattles, it rattled a warning.

An explosion of adrenaline shot through my body, causing me to leap up the remaining short distance of the walkway to the front door. I pressed the doorbell with a shaky finger as I kept looking behind me to make sure the snake was not following me. Not hearing any movement behind the door, I rang the bell again. No response. I tried knocking, with no success. No one was home. *Don't panic.*

The snake had not budged from the walkway, so I couldn't retrace my steps to the car. On either side of the walkway, large, wobbly-looking rocks filled the area between the house and the driveway. They seemed unstable, and the spaces between them were prime places for other snakes to be hiding. I picked up some pebbles that were next to the sidewalk and tossed one of them at the snake, hoping it would take the hint and move off the walkway. I missed the mark by about four inches. I tossed another pebble at the snake, hitting it in the tail. It rattled. I tried a third time, but that just made it angry. It rattled louder and coiled to strike, refusing to give up its sunbathing spot. I wondered if it could reach me from that distance—it wasn't very far. My fear ratcheted up a few notches and I could feel the blood pounding through my veins.

I fought to remain calm and considered my options. There was no other house nearby, so even if I called for help, no one would hear me. If I scrambled over the boulders on my right side and fell, I could break an ankle—or worse—and the snake could easily reach me. If I took the route on the left side I would still have to scramble over loose boulders and I would be even closer to the snake, but at least there would be a low wall between us. That was not much comfort, since I had read that snakes can climb over walls.

I chose the left side, took a deep breath, and hopped onto the most stable-looking rock as I kept one eye on the low wall that was separating me from the snake, while watching for snakes hiding between the boulders. I finally made it to my car, my legs wobbly with fear as I hurriedly unlocked the door and climbed inside. I sat there for a few minutes, waiting for the adrenaline rush to slow down so my heartbeat could return to normal. *That was a close one.*

Eventually, I calmed down enough to drive to the next house on my map. I wasn't far down the road when a black pig-looking animal streaked across right in front of my car. I slammed on the brakes and it took me a minute to realize what it was. A javelina, otherwise known as a peccary. I had never seen one before, but knew they were plentiful in this area. They looked similar to a wild boar and had sharp canine teeth that protruded from their mouths. *Be careful, Heidi.* I didn't want any more unpleasant surprises from the local wildlife. I finished the rest of my workday without incident and fell into bed that night, exhausted.

Eventually I developed a comfortable rhythm in Tucson, and sales were decent. Rylie and I took daily walks on a trail along a dry creek bed, where we could sometimes hear coyotes yipping off in the distance. I was invited to a happy hour at the campground and got to know some of my neighbors. Although there were no more close encounters with rattlesnakes, I did run into another javelina. It was lying next to a fence not far from the street when I was walking Rylie one morning. I knew that wild pigs could be dangerous and wasn't sure about javelinas. Rylie didn't know what to make of it. We quickly crossed to the other side of the street, just in case.

One week before the Canadian's scheduled visit, I received a voicemail message from him. I was attending an event at the RV park and had returned home late. I saw that he had called at nine p.m., and as I listened to his message, I could hear the sounds of driving, including the noise of a turn signal. He said he was at his house with his nephew, and they were going to watch a movie. I decided I would call him back the next day.

I phoned the Canadian the next evening, and he told me in great detail about the evening he had spent with his nephew, including the name of the movie they'd watched. His nephew was going to take care of his place while he came to visit me.

"Where did you go for dinner?" I asked.

"We didn't go out. Matthew came over about six p.m., and we had a pizza delivered. I showed him how to take care of things while I'm gone, and we stayed in all evening. He didn't leave until around eleven o'clock."

I felt my heart start beating double time. "You stayed in all evening? You didn't go out?"

"That's right. We were here all night."

"But your message . . ." My voice trailed off. An uncomfortable feeling started crawling over me.

"What about my message?"

"You left me a message at nine o'clock last night. You were driving."

There was a momentary silence on the phone. "No, I wasn't driving," he said, his voice quiet.

"But I heard car sounds. I could hear your turn signal in your message." I knew what I had heard in the background of his message. It was why I'd thought he had gone out to dinner. I knew he was lying, and my body knew it, too, because I suddenly felt weak. *Why would he lie about it? What was he doing that he doesn't want to tell me?* I remembered how he had been unable to talk to me as often recently because he said he was playing softball or otherwise busy. "What did you really do last night?"

"I told you, I was home with Matthew all night," he insisted.

"I know what I heard in your message."

"You're wrong."

"No, I'm not." It was my turn to talk quietly.

"I was home all night."

"Don't do this," I pleaded. "You're just making it worse."

"All I know is that I was home all night," he said stubbornly. We went back and forth like this a few more times, and suddenly, I was exhausted.

"I have to go," I said wearily. "I know you aren't being honest with me and haven't been for awhile." As soon as I said it, I realized this was true. I had felt for some time that he wasn't being truthful because of several small signs, but I'd never had any proof. Now I did. "I don't want you to come next week. I can't do this anymore. I need to be with someone I can trust. Goodbye." I hung up the phone, feelings of anger, sadness, and disgust swirling through me. Two minutes later, he called me back.

I answered the call but couldn't bring myself to say anything.

"Heidi, I'm sorry. I did go out, but I didn't want to tell you about it because I thought you would be upset. I met some friends at a bar."

"Why would I be upset about you going out with friends? Were you with a woman?"

"No, I just thought you might be upset, that's all."

That didn't make any sense. He must have thought I would be upset because he was on a date, but it didn't really matter to me what he had been doing. What mattered was that he had lied to me again. I knew I could never trust this man, no matter how much romance and appreciation he gave me. Romance dies if your partner can't be trusted.

"I can't see you or talk to you anymore," I said, starting to lay the bricks in the emotional wall. "It's over. I can't have a relationship with someone who lies to me. I hope you have a good life. Goodbye."

I hung up the phone, feeling nauseous. I crawled into bed and sobbed until Rylie jumped up on the bed and started licking my face, a concerned look in his eyes. I wrapped my arm around him and cried some more, until I finally fell asleep.

CHAPTER 34

REALITY CHECK

APRIL-JUNE 2009

*Heartbreak is hard, but you find more and more things
to be grateful for every day.*

—Olivia Culpo

T he next morning, I woke up with swollen eyes, feeling sick
to my stomach. This continued over the next several
weeks. *Why didn't I end the relationship after I found out he lied
about being divorced? How could I be such a fool?*

It didn't matter if the Canadian eventually left his wife. If
he couldn't be trusted to tell the truth, there would be no peace
in a relationship with him. There had been red flags that I
ignored, like the stolen tire cap and the story about playing
softball in the cold-weather months. I was clinging so
desperately to the romantic dream, I had put on my rose-
colored glasses and looked the other way. I wanted to believe
him when he told me I was special and that I was the only one
he wanted. I felt so appreciated in the spotlight of his love and
attention that I ignored the signs of decay on the sidelines.

I didn't just blame myself—I blamed the Canadian whole-
heartedly, and I hopscotched between anger and sadness. But I
recognized the part I'd played and that I was not without blame.

I thought I had turned my life around when I hit the road in my motorhome, but I had stumbled backward. I didn't realize I had more storms to weather and lessons to learn. *Two steps forward, one step back.*

Every time I turned on my laptop to check my email and I didn't see his name sitting in my inbox, sadness washed through me. I realized how much I'd looked forward to his emails, his phone calls, and his visits. They kept the occasional loneliness of traveling solo at bay. At first, this realization sent me spiraling into another depression. I lost my footing and was in a free fall. I was tired, listless, and lost. I went through the motions of working, but I wasn't having fun.

Then I got an email from a friend, who told me about Meetup, an online site that has social networking groups that meet in person for activities of all kinds. I decided to look up the groups in Tucson and found a salsa dancing group, so I joined it. That got me out meeting people, learning to salsa, and having fun. Soon, the nausea evaporated, and I began climbing out of the pit I had fallen into. I realized I was a smarter, stronger, more confident woman after this experience with the Canadian, and not as trusting.

It helped that I had a visitor to distract me. Lucy was going through Tucson, headed east. She stopped for a visit when I was planning to attend the Festival of Books, so she came along with me. We wandered around the festival, attending seminars, meeting authors, and buying books. I loved these events, and as a wannabe writer, I felt so inspired by what I saw and heard. I hoped this inspiration would finally spur me into action and I would write a book. I was good at starting them but not so great at finishing them. Lucy's positive outlook and quick humor brought some sunshine back to my mood, and with that and the inspiration from the book festival, I was feeling more like my new, happier self again.

I knew the Canadian was not the right man for me, but I started to have an appreciation for what we'd both gained through our relationship. He'd helped to bring out the fun, spontaneity, and passion in me that I had lost during my depression. He'd filled that empty space in my heart and made me feel beautiful. He'd given me the romance that I was craving, in abundance. I'd given him an escape from a loveless marriage, a variety of new travel adventures, and love. We'd both gotten something out of the relationship, even if it didn't end well.

By severing the connection once I realized his true nature, I also gained confidence. As painful as it was to let go, it made me stronger to take a stand for myself. I remembered the magic of the moment I had on the beach with the bioluminescence in the rain. That was a beautifully romantic moment with nature, and I was alone. I knew I didn't need a man to feel special.

I reluctantly left Tucson in early April. I was really starting to enjoy this city and would have been happy to stay longer. But I was excited to head to the Bay Area to celebrate Cammie's birthday. During the month I stayed there, I did a little bit of aerial photo work, but sales were not good. When it was time to go, I once again dragged my feet. Lately, it seemed, I wanted to linger more. But it was time to move on to Auburn, California, for more work.

Auburn was located about thirty miles northeast of Sacramento at the foot of the Sierra Nevada. It was surrounded by gentle, undulating hills, emerald forests, and sauntering rivers. It was garnished with a small, old-fashioned downtown area with some remnants from its gold rush past. A few weeks into my stay, I came out of my motorhome to see an Airstream trailer backing into the campsite next to mine. I was surprised to see an attractive woman in her early thirties get out of the truck with a little girl who looked to be about three years old.

After they got settled into their campsite, I walked over to say hello and introduced myself.

"Hi, Heidi. I'm Carol, and this is my daughter, Chloe."

"Hi, Chloe," I said. I looked at the tiny bundle of white fur she held clutched in her arms. "Who is this cute little furball?"

"This is Happy," Chloe said, coming closer so I could get a good look. "We call him that because he's always happy."

"Happy is a great name for a dog." I turned to Carol. "Where are you from?"

"We were from Texas, but we live in this now," Carol said, pointing to the Airstream trailer.

"You're a full-timer?" I asked with surprise. Carol was the first person I had met with a young child who lived and traveled in an RV. "I'm impressed. I can barely handle my motorhome and dog. I can't imagine managing a trailer, a dog, *and* a young child."

"I'm a single parent—it's always been just the two of us. I thought it would be fun to see the country while Chloe is little, and I can do my work from anywhere."

I marveled at this young, gutsy woman but didn't have much time to get to know her. A few days later, Carol, Chloe, and Happy hit the road again.

Although there were some blistering-hot days in Auburn, there was a nice trail along a canal that Rylie and I enjoyed walking every morning. My photo sales were good and I liked exploring the American River. It was a nice place to spend the summer, until the event I had feared most happened.

CHAPTER 35

THE FLOOD

JULY 2009

Too many of us are not living our dreams because we're living our fears.

—Les Brown

I stared at my flooded campsite, horror replacing annoyance as I realized it was not water that my motorhome was swimming in, but rather the overflowing contents of a blocked sewer system. Suddenly, I was no longer living the dream. This was a nightmare.

The entire time I traveled, this was the situation I'd feared most. Oddly, I was not particularly concerned about my motorhome breaking down in the middle of nowhere, whether I could get a job when I was ready to stop traveling, or even being the next victim of a serial killer. The situation that caused me the most anxiety was a sewage tank dumping gone awry. Although this was not because I'd dumped my sewage tanks, the result was the same.

My home on wheels carried two tanks: one for collecting the contents of the sinks and shower, known as the gray water tank, and the other for collecting the contents of the toilet, known as the black water tank. These tanks required at least weekly dumping—more often if I had visitors—into the sewer system of a campground or a dumping station.

I always approached this task with the apprehensive caution of a bomb squad approaching a ticking backpack. First, I donned a pair of extra-thick disposable gloves from the jumbo-sized box that I kept in the outside storage compartment at the tail end of the motorhome—the Hazard Zone. Next to the box of gloves was a large plastic storage bin with a protective cover, and inside of that, a heavy-duty trash bag—the kind that is capable of holding a small gorilla without breaking. Inside the trash bag were the nasty coils of sewer hoses and connections, objects I never handled without gloved hands and a wrinkled nose.

Next, I warily approached the exit valve for the RV tanks, the place where I attached my sewer hose and connector before opening the valve to allow the tank to empty into the sewer system. After I attached the connector and hose and tightened it three or four times, I checked and double-checked the connection. Then I put the other end of the sewer hose into the sewer drain of the campsite or dump station.

Sewer drains are not one size fits all, as I thought they would be. In fact, they come in a variety of sizes. Sometimes the drain opening was so small that my hose would barely fit. Other drains were so large that my hose was in danger of flying out of the drain at the slightest pressure from the emptying tanks. I went to great lengths to avoid this. The better dump stations sometimes had a heavy metal cover that held the sewer hose in place while the rushing contents emptied into the drain. For those times when there was no heavy cover to secure the hose, I carried a large block of cement, which I used to pin the hose in place with no hope of escape. This was my flying hose insurance.

Once I felt confident that the hose was securely fastened at both ends, I took a deep breath and gingerly opened the sewer tank valve micromillimeters at a time so as to avoid the sudden pressure of sewer contents that might launch the sewer hose and blast me with unspeakable horrors. Only when the last of the tank contents had trickled into the drain would I breathe a sigh of relief. *Another disaster averted.*

After that, the rest was easy. I opened the valve for the much less threatening gray water tank without anxiety. The gray water tank contents would rinse out the hose once, and then I would rinse it out a second time with a water hose. With the dreadful chore done for another week, I stowed everything in its covered, double-layer plastic home and packed it away out of sight. I would peel off my rubber gloves, folding them outside in, so as not to touch anything icky, and throw them in the trash. All was well until the next time I had to empty the tanks.

I wasn't the only RV traveler who approached this task with such dread. Annie wore thick rubber gloves—the type used for heavy-duty cleaning—and knee-high rubber boots every time she emptied her tanks, and still scrubbed herself vigorously with antibacterial wipes after removing her gloves.

Now, looking at the contents of the sewer system swirling around my camping chair and door mat, I would have given anything for a hazmat suit. When I'd arrived at this campground, I'd hooked up my sewer hose to the sewer drain valve in my campsite, and it had been securely fastened the entire time I was parked there. The sewer drain in a neighbor's campsite had overflowed because of some blockage in the sewer line, flooding their campsite and mine. I hurried over to the campground office.

"There's a sewage flood in my campsite," I informed the manager.

"I'm so sorry," the manager said. "I'll send a maintenance crew over there right away. They'll clean everything up."

I decided to take Rylie for a walk to get some fresh air until they were done with the cleanup. When I returned, the cleaners were rinsing things off with bleach and water, but I couldn't stomach the thought of sitting in my camp chair or setting foot on my mat. I donned a pair of disposable gloves, picked up my camp chair and mat, and tossed them in the trash.

Now that I had endured a sewage disaster and a broken heart, I knew I could handle whatever came my way. I was bouncing back quicker now, not as easily devastated by the curve balls life threw at me. They might slow me down from time to time, but I wasn't going to let things send me back to the dark place I'd been in before starting my journey. I was starting fresh, in more ways than one.

CHAPTER 36

WILDLIFE

AUGUST-OCTOBER 2009

*Your fears never go away. You just get more comfortable
ignoring them.*

—Jason Ritter

Except for the sewer disaster, I enjoyed my summer in
Auburn. I had visits from friends and family and also
made new friends in the campground and at some of the social
events I attended. I even had a couple of dates with men I met
through Meetup group activities, but there were no sparks.

Once my work was done, it was time to move on. I was
heading to Minnesota for another visit with my parents, with a
stop in Yellowstone National Park along the way. I had not
been to Yellowstone since I was a child, but I fondly
remembered the Old Faithful geyser, the excitement of seeing
wildlife, and the interesting, rustic architecture of the Old
Faithful Inn. I was eager to see this place we'd visited during
one of my childhood family vacations.

I was really hoping to see a moose in the wild and thought
Yellowstone might be a good place to see one. I saw a grizzly
bear, black bear, buffalo, elk, and coyote, but no moose. As I
took in the amazing and diverse scenery of this beautiful park,

there were times I wished I had someone to share in my experiences. Although I was meeting a lot of new people, it wasn't the same as having the companionship that comes with longtime friends or relationships. But I usually snapped out of my loneliness pretty quickly, and it didn't stop me from enjoying myself.

I hit the road again, heading for Minnesota. This was a working visit because I was going to help my parents get their house ready to sell. It was getting to be too much for them to take care of in their advancing age. I spent the next couple of weeks going through boxes, filling trash bins with unneeded things, and helping where I could.

When I was growing up, we knew there were bears around. They often got into trash cans, or we sometimes saw them running across the road when we were driving at dusk. In spite of all the time we spent playing in the woods, we never had any close encounters with bears, but I always feared them. I was told they could be unpredictable and dangerous, that they were fast runners and could climb trees, so I grew up afraid I might run into one.

While I was staying in Duluth, I took Rylie out for daily walks. There was a circular route we could take on the rural roads nearby. One day we were returning from our walk and only a couple hundred yards from my parents' house when Rylie suddenly stopped dead in his tracks and refused to budge.

I heard a crash in the woods, which were thick with brush on the right side of the road, then silence. I assumed it was a deer, which were plentiful here, galloping deeper into the forest. I started moving, but again Rylie refused to budge. I considered turning around and taking the long way back. I waited and listened, but I couldn't hear anything.

I started forward again, and this time Rylie came with me. Just as we were on top of the drainage pipe that ran beneath the road and fed water into a ditch alongside it, a bear popped its head out of the brush, about twenty-five feet from where we were. We looked right at each other, and I saw the surprise I felt mirrored on the bear's face. It had stopped to get a drink from the drainage ditch and was about to cross the road when it saw us. Adrenaline shot through my body, but I fought the urge to flee. *Don't run.*

I walked as fast as I could without running up the steep hill leading to my parents' house. When I was fifty feet away, I turned around to see if the bear was following us. It had come out to the middle of the road and stopped, watching us. When it saw me turn around, it suddenly loped across the road and into the woods on the other side. Once I realized I had nothing to fear from this curious bear, my body relaxed and my breathing returned to normal. As I approached my parents' house, I felt slightly exhilarated. I had come face-to-face with another longtime fear and made it through unscathed.

My mom was not so happy when I told her about it. "Here," she said a few days later, handing me a bear bell for Rylie to wear on his collar. "Make sure he wears that on all of your walks here." I didn't argue.

I planned to work the winter months in Florida but still had a couple of months before that work would be ready. From Minnesota, I went to Davenport, Iowa, for more work. I went from farm to farm, selling photos to very kind people with lots of cats. The cold temperatures stormed in early mid-October, so I decided to head down the map to chase a higher position on the thermometer. It was snowing my last day of work in Iowa, and my water hose froze that night. I was happy to put Iowa in my rearview mirror.

I was promised plenty of work in Beaumont, Texas, so I crawled south, stopping briefly in Saint Louis to spend the night. I entered the green, soggy state of Mississippi, planning to stop for the night in a state park near Grenada. After driving for miles on a winding backwoods road without seeing a soul, a prickly feeling started working its way up my spine. The sun was getting low in the sky, and I wanted to settle into my campsite before dark. I drove further, the woods thickening and closing in, and the sun slouching closer to the horizon. I began to wonder if I had somehow missed the turn for the campground. I would have turned around and gone back to the highway, but the road was narrow and there was no place where I could turn around without unhooking the car.

Just when I decided that I would have to stop and unhook the car so I could turn around, I was relieved to see the sign for the campground. My relief quickly disappeared when I looked around the deserted campsites. An ancient Winnebago was parked at the far end, draped with a blanket of fallen leaves and twigs. Faded curtains covered all of the windows, and there was no sign of life. There were no other campers and it was deadly silent. The hair on the back of my neck stood at attention, and I knew I had to get out of there. It just didn't feel right. I turned the motorhome around and made a hasty retreat to the exit. By the time I drove the many miles back to the highway, dusk was falling. I hightailed it up the highway and backtracked to another campground, where I managed to get parked before the inky night spilled down to the ground. It could have been unfounded fear that had me gunning to get out of that park; I will never know. But I was learning to pay attention to my intuition. Finally.

CHAPTER 37

TROUBLE KEEPS KNOCKING

OCTOBER 2009

If you could kick the person in the pants responsible for
most of your trouble, you wouldn't sit for a month.

—Theodore Roosevelt

I put Mississippi behind me and stopped for an uneventful night in Baton Rouge before arriving at my next work location in Beaumont, Texas. Beaumont is an oil town, with a very industrial feel to it. After getting settled in, I was having a hard time finding anything of interest to me there. My impression of the town may have been unfavorably colored by my experiences during the first couple of weeks I spent there. Nothing tragic or major happened, but rather a series of annoyances—like stepping in a dog turd.

Usually when I arrived at a new work location the photographer, pilot, and helicopter were long gone. The photography work was done, and the photos were ready to sell when I arrived. That was not the case in Beaumont. Because of scheduling problems with the photographer, mistakes made by the office, and delays due to weather, my work in Beaumont wouldn't start for about two weeks.

That probably would not have bothered me if I had been just about anywhere other than Beaumont. As far as I could tell, there wasn't much of anything to do there, and it rained in sheets. The RV park was flooded, including my campsite. The grassy patch between the campsites sat in two inches of water because the ground was so saturated, there was nowhere for it to go. Rylie and I couldn't get into the motorhome without walking through mud, so I moved it slightly the next day so the door was in front of a smaller mud puddle and parked my car in a different spot so that I could avoid walking through the worst of the mud. It was getting pretty dirty inside, despite my best efforts to keep my feet and Rylie's paws clean.

I don't know whether it was from all of the rain or the electrical service at the RV park, but one day when I was outside the motorhome dumping the tanks, I noticed that the yellow electrical cord had turned black. I looked closer and saw that it was burned. I reported it to the RV park management, but they insisted everything was okay with the electrical system. I bought a new electrical cord and hoped for the best.

Rylie still needed to be walked, no matter the weather. For the first few days, we arrived back at the motorhome completely soaked following our brief dashes outside, just long enough for Rylie to do his business. Finally, the downpour stopped and we could venture outside the boundaries of the RV park for a longer stroll. Mud oozed in a gooey layer on top of the roads and sidewalks from the flooding. I did my best to avoid it, but sometimes I couldn't help stepping in it. In one spot my feet hit the mud and skated ahead at top speed, then decided to try flying. As my legs went into the air, I landed hard on my back, banging my head on the concrete. Although I had a royal headache and a sore back, I was lucky I wasn't knocked unconscious—or worse. Once again, I worried about what would happen to Rylie if something bad happened to me.

After that, I was more careful during our walks. But that wasn't the end of my bad luck run.

I decided to catch up on some of my housekeeping and maintenance chores when the rain stopped. I started by washing my screens and then climbed up on the roof of the motorhome to wash off my vent lids. As I did, I poked a hole in the plastic of one of the lids. Being exposed to the sun and other elements had deteriorated the plastic so much that it crumbled at my touch. It had to be repaired immediately, otherwise the next rain would come right through the screen into the motorhome. I found a place in Beaumont that did RV repairs, and they had one in stock. I climbed back up on the roof and replaced the vent lid, but the Green Monster still wasn't happy.

The water heater wouldn't start any time it rained. Another day my car had problems starting, resulting in hundreds of dollars of repairs. Then I got a nail in my car tire, my GPS stopped working, a rock hit the motorhome windshield and damaged it in two places, and I got the stomach flu. When I got over that, I stepped outside the motorhome onto the grassy patch between campsites, landing smack-dab on an anthill, and my sandal-clad foot was immediately attacked by fire ants. This all happened during the span of two weeks. I couldn't wait to get back to work.

Finally, the photos were ready. I was working in a rural part of Beaumont and walked up to the door of a home that had a border collie roaming loose. The dog barked at me a couple of times but didn't seem like a real threat. As I reached out to ring the doorbell, the dog snuck up behind me and nipped me in the leg. It barely broke the skin but later produced a healthy bruise. That was the first and only time I was ever bitten on that job, which was surprising, considering the number of homes with loose dogs that I visited. The frosting on this cake of minor catastrophes was when I actually did step on a dog turd.

This barrage of bad luck could have upset or depressed me, and probably would have in my previous life. But the continual string of annoyances got so ridiculous, I just got the giggles. There was nothing I could do; I just had to deal with it. But I didn't let it send me into a dark funk. This was huge progress for me.

There was a silver lining to this canker-sore cloud. I got to go for a helicopter ride. My manager wanted to do something nice since I had to wait so long to start work, so he arranged it with the pilot. The helicopter was really tiny, a Robinson R22, and it barely fit two people. We flew with my door off, which made me really grateful for the seat belt. Something about that open-air feeling had me imagining that I was flying like Superman. The pilot decided to give me a thrill and cut the engine. He said we were falling at fifteen hundred feet per minute, but it felt like we were merely drifting down, like a hot-air balloon. I wasn't scared but did have a brief moment when I wondered if the helicopter would start again. We landed safely on the ground and I was happy to check "helicopter ride" off my bucket list.

During my downtime I also got to explore nearby places, such as Galveston and Orange. Then I took a break and drove to New Orleans to meet up with Lucy, Annie, and Karen for Halloween. We met at an RV park and when I arrived, Lucy and Karen were already parked. We exchanged greetings and hugs and sat in our camp chairs to catch up.

"Annie is staying at the house she inherited from her aunt," Lucy said. "She's on her way here."

"Great, I'm so happy to see both of you," I said, and meant it.

"Have you been to New Orleans before?" Lucy asked.

"No, this is my first time," I replied. "I've always wanted to come here, and Halloween should be a fun time to visit. Have you both been here before?"

"I've been here a couple of times," Lucy said. "I know a few good places to go."

"This is my first time," Karen said. "I bet Annie has some good suggestions, too, since she stays here a lot now."

A short time later, Annie pulled up and asked, "Would you like a little tour of New Orleans?" She showed us the beautiful mansions of the Garden District and pointed out Hurricane Katrina's devastating remnants throughout the city, although the rebuilding had been going on for years. This was a city of survivors who didn't give up. Annie brought us to the house she now owned, and we did a tour of the famous Saint Louis Cemetery. We also walked the streets of the French Quarter, where something interesting was always happening.

New Orleans captured my heart. It was filled with art, history, beautiful architecture, and unique culture. I could identify with its adventurous and independent spirit. The food was delicious, and oh, the music. In the French Quarter musicians were in every other restaurant and bar, on street corners, and in the parks. Music was everywhere.

On Halloween, we went to the French Quarter. I love Halloween, and this was the best Halloween party I have ever seen. The streets were packed with people outfitted in creative and colorful costumes. There was also a Mardi Gras-style parade, although on a much smaller scale.

The best part was having a reunion with Lucy, Annie, and Karen. I felt a renewed fondness for these adventurous, independent women. I thought back to the months before I went to Baja with Lucy, Karen, and Elaine and how nervous I had been about fitting in with these incredible women. I laughed inwardly at how silly my unfounded fears were, grateful that I had decided to go anyway and gotten to spend time with these friends.

CHAPTER 38

ALLIGATOR COUNTRY

DECEMBER 2009-MARCH 2010

Writing is the hardest way of earning a living, with the possible exception of wrestling alligators.

—Olin Miller

After all of the trouble in Beaumont, I was really happy to head over to Florida, where I would spend the winter working. I heaved a sigh of relief as I passed the city limits of Beaumont. Except for the trips I had taken to other cities, I had not enjoyed my time in Texas. I had never been to Florida, so I was eager to explore a new state.

Cammie was flying to Tampa to spend the Christmas holiday with me, and I could barely contain my excitement. I got settled into an RV park in Punta Gorda, which was on the gulf side between Tampa and Fort Myers, and started researching things we could do while she was visiting. This was also Cammie's first time in Florida and I looked forward to discovering it with her.

"What do you want to do while you're in Florida?" I asked Cammie after I picked her up at the airport and got her settled in the motorhome.

"I want to see some alligators," she said.

"Good, me too. I heard that Alligator Alley near the Everglades is a good place to see them. Why don't we go there?"

Cammie agreed, so the next day, we drove an hour and a half to the H. P. Williams Roadside Park on Highway 41. We saw some alligators on the far side of the canal at this stop, but it was really wide here. They were too far away and camouflaged in the tangle of trees and bushes that flanked the water.

I saw an unassuming dirt road skirting the nearer side of the canal. "Let's see where that road goes," I said as we got into the car. That little dirt road led us to the alligator jackpot. The canal was narrower here, so the alligators sunning themselves on the other side were much closer, and there were lots of them. More were swimming in the water further away. We pulled over right next to the canal, and there was nothing between us and the water except for a small patch of grass and weeds.

"Don't get too close," I warned Cammie. "Alligators can be dangerous. They're sneaky and move really fast."

We parked the car alongside the road and got out to take photos of the alligators sunbathing on the far side of the canal. These large, prehistoric-looking creatures were as still as statues and often didn't look real. Every once in a while, we would see some movement, or one would slide into the water. We even saw some furious splashing with legs and tails flailing about and wondered whether the alligators were fighting or feeding on something.

We were standing next to the car snapping photos within ten feet of the water when an alligator suddenly burst to the surface, right in front of us. We had not seen it swimming toward us, and there had been no disturbance in the water until it flung itself into sight. We both jumped and made a hasty retreat into the car. We kept our distance after that, but we felt lucky to see dozens of alligators that day and got some great photos.

Back at the motorhome I asked Cammie, "Would you like to go see the manatees? We've never seen one of those."

"Sure!" Cammie was enthusiastic. She liked seeing wildlife as much as I did.

I made arrangements for a boat trip to see the manatees on another day. On the day of the reservation we drove to Fort Myers to take a boat tour on the muddy-watered Orange River. When the water temperature in the Gulf of Mexico creeps below 68 degrees, the manatees migrate to the more hospitable waters of the rivers, where the temperature is warmer. They especially like where the power plant releases warm water into the Orange River, creating a spa-like atmosphere. Manatees don't come out of the water like whales do, so they are harder to see. There is no breaching, spy-hopping, or blowing of spray. Manatees glide up to the surface at a glacial pace for a quiet grab of air, with only their bulky, pale shape beneath the surface and a quick glimpse of gray snout to give their presence away. This made it nearly impossible to photograph them, but we enjoyed what little we could see of these easygoing blobs just below the surface.

I soaked up the much-needed mother-daughter time with Cammie. The longer my travels went on, the more I realized how much I missed her. When our Christmas holiday together was over, I watched with a heavy heart as she disappeared into the airport terminal to catch her flight back to California. This travel adventure, as good as it was for my soul, came at a cost.

I consoled myself with the knowledge that my parents would be visiting in a couple of weeks. This would be their first visit to Florida too, and their first time staying in the motorhome. I thought my parents would be as thrilled to see alligators as Cammie and I had been, but my mom seemed nervous at the lack of barriers between us and the alligators. My dad, who was legally blind from macular degeneration but had a little bit of sight, couldn't distinguish the alligators from the canal banks and trees surrounding them. I decided to try Sanibel Island next, thinking they would enjoy the beautiful beaches and quaint restaurants that sprinkled the island.

Sanibel has a wildlife drive densely populated with wintering birds. I don't think my dad saw much, but my mom and I saw spoonbills, anhingas, white ibises, great egrets, cormorants, and even an osprey along this wing-filled drive. There were many other birds that I couldn't identify. I wanted to see what one of the beaches looked like, and my parents reluctantly followed me on the short walk to the beach so I could snap a few photos. We found a place to have lunch on the island after that. I don't think my parents enjoyed the wildlife and scenery of Florida as much as I did, but it was still nice to spend time together.

After my parents returned to Minnesota, I got back to work, but I also revved up my social life. I joined some Meetup groups, including a social group that met for a variety of fun activities. I attended lunches and dinners, swing and salsa dance lessons, and even started dating a member of the group. I joined a writing group and struck up a conversation with Aaron, one of the members.

"You should check into writing articles for Examiner.com," Aaron said after one of our meetings. "It's an online news source and it's a good way to get published. All you need to do is submit a writing sample and get approved, and you can start publishing articles online. If you get enough of a following, you can make some money."

After our next meeting, I went over to Aaron. "Thanks for telling me about Examiner. I sent in my writing sample and got approved. I am now an RV travel examiner."

"Congratulations!" Aaron said. "Now you can practice your writing skills and get articles published at the same time. I'm going to do it too, although I'm not sure yet what I'll write about."

Since my only online writing experience was my blog, I considered it good for honing my writing skills. I published more than fifty articles but never gained enough readers to make any real money.

As I settled into my Florida work and social routine, I thought the Green Monster had entered a quiet state of happiness, but it started complaining before long. It was the water pump again. I did some research to find out which water pump models were supposed to be good, then called Jim, an RV technician, and told him the specific one I wanted. "Can you install this model water pump for me?" I asked.

"Sure, no problem," Jim said. "I can be there the day after tomorrow." While he was installing the pump, I happened to look over at the discarded box that the new pump came in.

"Jim, that's not the correct model water pump," I said. "I asked for that particular model because reviews said the other models weren't as good." I didn't want to have yet another leaky water pump, after going through this twice already.

"No problem, I'll go get the right one." He left and returned a short time later with the right model, got it installed, and left. A few hours later, I discovered another leak, but it wasn't the pump. It hadn't been installed correctly. I called Jim.

"Jim, I don't think the pump is installed correctly. It's leaking at the connection."

"I'll be there in a couple of hours," he said. He came and reinstalled the pump, fixing the leak. After that, the Green Monster settled down again and I had no further problems with the water pump.

My plan was to visit the Florida Keys after my work was done and then head north to explore the East Coast, but I received an offer I couldn't refuse. It was a four-month contract job doing instructional design work for a consulting company, and it paid well. Photo sales had not been the best in Florida, because of the real estate market crash and skyrocketing number of foreclosures. Although I was having a fun social life in Florida, I decided to accept this offer and cut my Florida visit short. I didn't feel a strong emotional connection to the man I was dating, and I don't think he felt a strong connection with me, so it wasn't difficult to say goodbye. After my experience with the Canadian, I was pretty cautious. I no longer jumped right into a relationship with my heart in my hand, ready to offer it at the first sign of romance. I was finally learning to take my time and refuse to be rushed.

CHAPTER 39

BACK TO THE WILD WEST

APRIL-JULY 2010

Every parting is a form of death, as every reunion is a type of heaven.

—Tryon Edwards

My plans for exploring the rest of Florida and the northeast part of the country were scrapped. I was required to be on-site in Las Vegas for the first month of the instructional design project, but then I could telecommute. I did manage to squeeze in a quick visit to St. Augustine before scuttling across the country to Vegas. It was a little out of the way, but I couldn't go that far east and not see the Atlantic Ocean, and I wanted to see this city.

St. Augustine is the oldest city in the country and is filled with historic buildings and cute cobblestone streets in a pedestrian mall. As I toured the fort, climbed to the top of the lighthouse, and poked around in the shops, I grew really fond of this city. I was hoping to camp in Anastasia State Park, but the campground was full. The Florida state park campgrounds book up about a year in advance and many of the private campgrounds are really expensive. I felt lucky to find a decent campground for $30 a night that was only four miles from Old Town, the historic part of the city.

I only had a week to get to Las Vegas before starting work, so there would not be much sightseeing on this trip. I did a quick stop in New Orleans and visited a couple of plantations in the River Road area. I had never seen a plantation, so I toured two of them on that scenic drive. Strangely, one of the plantations had seemingly erased any evidence of slavery, as though it never happened. The other plantation didn't try to sweep it under the rug, but instead included in the tour the slave quarters and other information about that terrible dark age of our history.

I did a quick hop over the rest of the country and got settled into an RV park in Las Vegas, but it was the most expensive place I had ever stayed. There weren't many choices available. I got a bit of a break with the monthly rate, but this place still gave me the biggest sticker shock I had while traveling.

Although I was happy for the work in Las Vegas, it was difficult getting used to waking up before six a.m. and going to work in an office again. I missed the freedom of setting my own schedule, and I felt guilty leaving Rylie in the motorhome while I was at work, even if he was in air-conditioned comfort. But I needed to make more money. I hadn't been saving for retirement while traveling, so unless I wanted to work until I died, I had to get my bank balance going in the right direction. When the alarm went off each morning, I reminded myself I was getting paid a lot more than I was making with my photo sales, and it was good experience. After working a month in the office, I could work from the motorhome and wouldn't have to get up quite so early. I could stay home with Rylie and work in my pajamas if I wanted to, although I always had to get up and walk Rylie before working, so I opted for sweatpants.

The month went by quickly, then I made my way back to the Bay Area, after a stop at the motorhome manufacturer in Southern California for some repairs. The Green Monster was clamoring for attention once again, and when I got to the Bay Area, it would need new tires. Although the tread was still good on the tires, they were now four years old and starting to crack. Between the car and the motorhome, it seemed there was always something needing maintenance, repair, or replacement.

There weren't any strictly RV parks or campgrounds near Cammie, but there were a few mixed mobile home and RV places. I found a spot in the nicest park, in Pleasant Hill, with big trees, a reasonable monthly rate, and a nice trail nearby for walking. Now that I was telecommuting, I needed to stay in a place where I could get fast internet, and this place had cable.

I had not seen Cammie since the Christmas holidays, and it was early May. I was really missing her. She had a new boyfriend, and I had fun spending time with them, and also catching up with friends. Although I really enjoyed Florida, Las Vegas was not my kind of place. It felt really good to be back in California.

My contract work got extended an extra month, so I stayed in the Bay Area and worked through August. I joined a hiking group and spent a lot of my free time walking and socializing with my new friends. I was having fun. It became clear to me that as much as I'd enjoyed the travel and freedom of the past few years, I missed being close to family and friends.

After my contract work ended the Green Monster started complaining again. The house batteries were not holding a charge, according to the battery monitor, so I replaced them. But that didn't satisfy the temperamental Green Monster. I called an RV technician out, and I was told it was a converter issue. I shelled out more money.

I reflected on the many repairs I'd had while traveling. That was the thing about this lifestyle that caused me the most heartburn. I did not have good mechanical skills, which meant that I had to rely on the local RV repair technicians. I always felt like I had to do a lot of research on the internet and calling around to figure out what should be done and which brand of parts to buy, and then check prices. On more than one occasion I had technicians who tried to overcharge me, but I would not have known that if I had not checked into the customary prices. Perhaps they thought I was a dumb woman who wouldn't know any better, but I learned that it paid to do my own research. Although I still did not have enough knowledge and experience to do some of the repairs myself, I was more confident about dealing with repair issues.

After the repairs were done I headed to the Eastern Sierra for a reunion with Lucy, Karen, and Elaine at a camping get-together with a bunch of women who owned Lazy Daze motorhomes. We stayed at a Bureau of Land Management campground along Highway 395 in Lone Pine, California. The campground was near the Eastern Sierras and the Alabama Hills, a popular filming spot for television shows and movies, especially westerns. Mount Whitney was a towering sentinel in the beautiful background to the campsites. The stark contrast between the dusty desert scrub of the campground snuggled against the backdrop of this king of the mountains—the highest peak in the continental United States—was strikingly dramatic. We reminisced about our time on the Baja Peninsula, and I longed for that carefree time when I wasn't working and could do whatever I wanted.

After a few days of laughs, wine tasting, and seeing the local sights, the event was over. Lucy and I headed to nearby Yosemite National Park and camped in Tuolumne Meadows. Lucy wasn't a hiker, so I did a solo hike to the top of Lembert Dome and was rewarded with a beautiful view across the valley. If my bank balance hadn't been complaining, I would have liked to stay longer in the park and explore more of it.

There was much more to see, but it was time to slip back into my work harness.

Once again, I felt a pang of sadness as I said goodbye to Lucy. I had so much fun with this fearless woman who always made me laugh, and I wasn't sure when we would meet up again. I made my way up the highway to Carson City, Nevada, for my next photo sales assignment. I stopped on the way to visit Bodie, which claims to be the best-preserved ghost town in the country. Unfortunately, the never-ending, bumpy road was not well preserved, and my shock absorbers died somewhere along the way. I cursed the Green Monster.

CHAPTER 40

GROWING DISENCHANTMENT

OCTOBER 2010-FEBRUARY 2011

*Disenchantment, whether it is a minor disappointment
or a major shock, is the signal that things are moving into
transition in our lives.*

—William Throsby Bridges

I was miserable. I had just spent two months in humid
middle-of-nowhere Texas and a lonely Thanksgiving. This
was the third work assignment I'd had in Texas, and I decided I
just wasn't a Texas kind of person. The sales were better in
Texas than Carson City, Nevada, where I'd just spent two
months, but I wanted out of Texas.

My solitary, nomadic lifestyle had become more of a chore
than an adventure. It would have been different if I didn't have
to work and could have traveled wherever I wanted, or if I had
a partner to share the journey and experience with. I missed
having an established circle of friends that I could call if I
wanted company for a movie, walk, or meal.

I'd had that for a couple of months before heading to
Texas. Chantay, whom I'd met in Pahrump and occasionally
ran into along my travels, could work from anywhere, so she
joined me in Carson City. We stayed at the same RV park and

socialized after work. We had fun together, but after a couple of months of tepid sales and not much to do, I had to make a change.

"I'm going to follow my boss's suggestion to try Texas," I told Chantay. "Photo sales are usually better in Texas, and they have photos in a small town about fifty miles from Houston."

"I don't want to go to Texas," Chantay said. "I'm heading back to Las Vegas." We hugged each other goodbye and agreed to meet up again somewhere down the road. I headed to Texas but soon began to regret my decision, even if I was making more money.

Two job offers arrived and allowed me to escape from Texas. One was another short-term contract job doing instructional design work. The other was a very part-time gig doing freelance writing for an RV tour company. The best part was, I could work from the motorhome for both jobs, as long as I had an internet connection. I called Cammie.

"Guess what? I'm coming back for Christmas, and I get to stay for a while!"

"Yay!" she cheered. "How soon will you be here?"

"I need to stop in Southern California to get the electric step repaired and fix the wiring on the tow bar, but I should be there next week." I was really tired of the Green Monster's demands constantly raiding my wallet. Still, when I considered what I would have paid in rent or a mortgage in California, it wasn't that bad.

I settled into my old trailer park spot in Pleasant Hill to hunker down for my fifth winter in the motorhome. I hired the local handyman to modify my propane line so that I could hook up an external propane tank. They didn't deliver propane where I was staying, so I got a smaller, external tank that I could get filled at the hardware store. That made life easier and was well worth the small amount of money it cost for the work.

One day in late January, I was vacuuming in the bedroom of the motorhome when I saw a portion of a tooth lying on the carpet. I knew it wasn't mine, so I called Rylie over to have a look in his mouth. Sure enough, he had broken one of his molars, most likely on the synthetic bone he sometimes chewed. Rylie rarely got sick or injured and never complained when he did. I brought him in to the vet, who looked into his mouth and quickly gave his opinion.

"The pulp of the tooth is exposed, so I recommend removing the rest of the tooth to prevent infection. It should be done soon."

"What's involved with that?" I asked.

"We'll need to give him general anesthesia in order to get the tooth out. Since we're doing that, we should probably clean the rest of his teeth."

I made the appointment for two days later and fed him the recommended soft foods. On the morning of Rylie's dental surgery, I pulled into the parking lot of the veterinary hospital and opened the passenger door. Rylie hopped out of the front seat, took one look at where we were, then hopped right back into the car and got into the backseat. I managed to get him out of the car, but he kept trying to go in the opposite direction. Poor little guy was trembling with fear by the time we got inside. He hated going to the vet.

"We'll keep him all day so we can make sure he's okay and give him another pain shot before he goes home. You can pick him up after five o'clock," the assistant said as she took his leash from me.

"It's okay, I'll come to get you later," I reassured Rylie as she led him to the back. I felt the guilty and conflicted pangs of a mother turning her child over for a painful but necessary medical procedure.

When I returned at the appointed time, the assistant walked Rylie slowly down the hall to the reception desk.

There was no wagging tail and no smiling face. This was the only time in our ten years together that he had not been happy to see me. I lifted him carefully into the passenger seat of the car, where he usually sat while I was driving. As we drove back to the motorhome, I repeatedly looked at him to make sure he was okay. He kept his back to me the entire ride home, something he had never, ever done. It was very clear that I was in the doghouse.

It was a bad night. Rylie whined and paced, so I knew he was really hurting. He was always a stoic and usually didn't yelp, whine, or cry when he was hurt. I gave him the pain medication on schedule, but it didn't seem to help much. I called the vet's office first thing in the morning, and they advised me to increase the frequency of the medication. He was much better the following day, and I breathed a sigh of relief. I was more dependent on my trusty little companion than I'd realized, and I couldn't imagine doing this journey without him. Seeing him suffer was much worse than if I'd endured the procedure myself. I felt the same way whenever Cammie was sick or in pain. After a few days we settled back into our usual routine.

Winters were tough in the confined space of a motorhome, when the rain and cold kept us inside most of the time, and I found myself getting cabin fever more often. *I need to get out of this tin can.* I finished my instructional design work in late February, so I decided to beat my winter blues by taking a trip to the island of Hawaii. Rylie was completely recovered from his dental surgery and stayed with Cammie while I was gone, so I didn't need to worry about him.

Hawaii was good medicine. I soaked up as much sunshine as my fair skin would allow without burning, which wasn't much. I took a drive around the island, went to Hawai'i Volcanoes National Park, snorkeled, saw the Place of Refuge, and drank mai tais on the lanai while watching the distant spray of whales in the ocean. One day, I was swimming at Hapuna Beach when a big sea turtle swam nearby. It felt so good to be out of the cramped motorhome, I didn't want my Hawaii vacation to end. I reluctantly boarded the plane to head back to the motorhome.

CHAPTER 41

THE GATHERING CLOUDS

MARCH-JUNE 2011

To us, family means putting your arms around each other and being there.

—Barbara Bush

"We're having an RV rally in Pahrump and would like you to come and get to know the people and events so you can write for us. Are you available?" My freelance writing client was on the phone. I had responded to an ad on Craigs List for a freelance writer working for an RV travel company and, after a phone interview and submitting a writing sample, I was hired.

My parents were planning to visit Las Vegas for a month, and Pahrump was only an hour away. I could combine attending the rally and a visit with my parents. "Sure, I'd love to come." After the months I'd spent in Pahrump peddling photos, I never thought I would return, but this was a good opportunity to meet the client and see what their rallies were like.

After Vegas and Pahrump I returned to California, but the Central Valley this time. I was doing more photo sales in Visalia, where orange orchards were intertwined with dairy farms. It felt like a small town, even though the population was 125,000. Photo sales were good, so I decided to stay for a few months. I hadn't expected much from this town, but I was pleasantly surprised. Visalia had more to offer than I'd thought.

Chantay decided to join me there, and we found a local hangout called Crawdaddy's that had good food and excellent music. Every Sunday evening, they had a jam session where various musicians would show up to play or sing. Some of them were really talented. We became Sunday regulars, having dinner and a glass or two of wine, and enjoying the music. Sometimes we even got up and danced.

We sampled the restaurants in town, some of which were quite good. One day we were strolling by the downtown shops, and something in one of the store windows caught my eye, stopping me in my tracks. It was a set of whimsical, brightly colored dinnerware.

"Let's go in here," I said as I entered the store and made a beeline for the dishes. I don't know why, but I was smitten. Looking at those dishes with the flowers and butterflies just made me feel happy.

"These breakable dishes make no sense for someone living in a motorhome, but I want them," I told Chantay. "I think I'm tired of eating off plastic dishes." I had sold or given away my stuff when I sold my house and bought the motorhome, and it had been a freeing experience. I was glad to be rid of the weight of all of those possessions that had tied me down to one place. But suddenly, I wanted a full set of real dishes again. Not the sturdy, unbreakable dishes suitable for a motorhome. I wanted dishes that would chip or break—pretty dishes. Ones that would look good on a real table in a real home. *This doesn't make any sense.* Then the realization burst into my consciousness: *I'm done.* I wanted something more permanent. I was ready to end my journey and settle down in one place again.

I thought about what had started me on this journey, the depression that had me envying the freedom of the homeless. I had changed and was no longer depressed, but why? Was it simply having some time and freedom to do as I pleased and reconnect with myself? Or was it escaping from the confines of chasing the conventional American Dream? I didn't know, but I was grateful for having this experience.

"I'll take the whole set," I told the store clerk. "But please wrap them carefully and put them in boxes so they won't break." I loaded the dishes in the trunk of my car, where they wouldn't be jostled and could wait for the next chapter in my life.

"I'm ready to settle down again," I told Chantay. "Now I need to find a permanent, full-time job." I started searching for jobs on Craigslist. I applied for a few instructional designer jobs with consulting companies but got no response, other than the automatic email replies that are so common now. I continued peddling aerial photos.

One day, Chantay and I took a drive to Sequoia National Park to see the giant trees. Although it was the middle of May, snowdrifts dotted the ground as we entered the park. A light rain began to fall as we entered the visitor center, so we decided it wasn't a good day for hiking.

We wandered along the short trail to see the General Sherman tree, the largest tree in the world by volume. I stood in front of this 275-foot tree as Chantay took my picture and felt incredibly tiny. I loved the fresh, clean air among these trees, and the quiet woods made me feel peaceful and rejuvenated. I felt just as much at home here as I had on the beach in Baja. *I can fit in many different places.*

One Sunday evening, Chantay and I were having an especially good time enjoying the music at Crawdaddy's, when I was suddenly overcome by overwhelming feelings of sadness and loss. I didn't know where the feelings had come from or why they'd hit me all of a sudden. I turned to look at Chantay.

"We need to hang on to this moment," I told her. "You never know what might be lurking right around the corner."

"Okay." Chantay smiled at me, as if she thought the wine had gone to my head. That wasn't the reason for my sudden sadness, but since I couldn't explain it, I was silent.

Not long after that, I received a phone call from my Mom.

"Your dad went to the doctor and they ran some tests. He has colon cancer."

"Oh no, how bad is it?" I remembered the feeling I'd had at Crawdaddy's that night. Maybe it was a premonition, because trouble had arrived. I wasn't surprised that my dad had a health issue. He had endured two serious infections in his heart, radiation for prostate cancer, and a quintuple bypass surgery.

"They want to do surgery to take out part of his colon, but they think they can get it all." She was trying to reassure me, but I could tell my mom was worried. She was always worrying about someone.

"Try not to worry, Mom. He's a tough guy. He survived all of that other stuff, he can beat this too."

"Oh yes, I'm sure he'll be fine." Mom always tried to stay positive, despite her worrying nature.

Then I talked to my dad, who seemed to take it all in stride with his usual bluntness.

"They're going to cut out the bad stuff in the colon, but it shouldn't be too bad. I'm not worried."

"That's good, because worrying doesn't help. I can come back there for a couple of weeks. Would you rather I come for the surgery or for your birthday?" My dad's birthday was a few weeks following the surgery.

"Come for my birthday. There's going to be lots of people here for the surgery." Both of my sisters and my brother were planning to be there for the surgery, so my parents would be well supported. I made my flight arrangements to be there a few weeks later, in early July. Flying instead of driving would give me more time to spend with my parents.

As I was finishing up my sales work near Visalia, something happened that had a profound effect on me and that I would remember for years to come. I stopped at a dairy farm to show them an aerial photo that we had of the farm. I walked from building to building, trying to find someone to talk to, but all I could see were pens filled with cows. Finally, I saw a worker and asked if the owner or manager was around. He pointed off in the distance, where a man was driving a tractor in our direction. I started walking to meet the tractor, which stopped. A young man hopped off and walked quickly toward me. I introduced myself and told him why I was there.

"Come back tomorrow morning," he said. "The owner will be here then. I'm sure he would like to see it." I thanked him and told him I would be back in the morning, then started walking back to my car. He drove the tractor past the corralled cows as I was walking, and it was only then that I could see that he was dragging a dead cow behind the tractor.

As the manager drove past the cows, a few of them began to follow, then run frantically alongside the dragged cow. I had never seen cows run like that. They were clearly distressed at seeing the dead cow being dragged behind the tractor. Grief was written all over them. Humans are not the only ones who suffer and grieve.

After working in triple-digit temperatures, I was ready to leave Visalia. My car had been complaining, and the resulting repairs had left an echo in my wallet. It was time to go. Chantay was headed to Southern California, so we hugged each other goodbye and agreed to stay in touch. I drove back to the Bay Area to get Rylie settled in at Cammie's house before I flew to Minnesota.

CHAPTER 42

FULL CIRCLE

JULY-NOVEMBER 2011

The wheel is come full circle.

—William Shakespeare

I flew to Minnesota and got a rental car at the airport. My dad was in his usual position when I got to the house: prone on the couch. Whenever I think of my dad over the past four decades, he is always lying on the couch. It may have started when I was very young, after his back surgery, but from the earliest time I can remember, it was always this way. He would lie there to watch television and read the paper, his usual evening activities at home. Occasionally, he would sit up to eat if someone brought him a sandwich, peanuts, or some ice cream.

"How are you, Dad?"

"Oh, I'm getting there." He sat up and gave me a hug. "Glad I'm not in that hospital. I couldn't get any rest there. They were always waking me up for something—taking my temperature and giving me pills."

"You are one tough guy."

"I guess so. I never thought I would still be alive at this age."

"You're a survivor," I said. "You've lived through a lot."

Those two weeks were some of the sweetest I could remember spending with my parents in recent years. I felt a new tenderness for my dad that I hadn't known before, because I'd had such mixed feelings about him when I was growing up. I had been angry with him when I was a teenager, for the way his drinking and absence had damaged our family, and it took many years for me to forgive him. Now I saw the frailty in this man I'd always seen as strong willed and fiercely independent. Although he'd eventually quit drinking and smoking, his hard-living ways had caught up with his body. He loved his family, though. I could see that clearly now. It had taken a very long time, but I was able to forgive my dad for the hurt his drinking and behavior caused me, my mom, and the rest of the family.

That summer in Duluth had other sweet gifts. One night, I got to experience two of my favorite Minnesota summer hallmarks. It was after sunset, and I could feel the weight of the air through the open windows, heavy with humidity. I looked out to see tiny, blinking green lanterns flitting about the night sky. Fireflies. When I was young, I thought they were magical. As I watched them all of these years later, I still thought so.

A short time later, I heard distant rumblings, gradually moving closer. Then a streak of lightning crackled across the sky, followed by the crashing staccato of more thunder, louder. More bolts of light and ear-splitting pounding, gradually softening as the storm moved off to the next audience. I missed thunder and lightning storms, because we rarely got them in the Bay Area. I'd seen a few during my travels, but they didn't seem as dramatic as the Minnesota thunderstorms. Family, fireflies, and lightning—some of the best things about Minnesota summers.

Halfway through my visit, I received a phone call. It was one of the consulting companies I'd applied with for instructional design work. They wanted me to come in for an interview in the Bay Area. I told them I would be returning in about a week, so we scheduled a face-to-face interview for shortly thereafter.

To help my parents get their home ready to sell I went through boxes, sorting the contents into piles that could be discarded, sold, or donated. I had a painting marathon in the living room, dining room, and hallway that I barely finished before it was time to catch my flight to California. My parents were putting their house on the market soon. They had lived in the house for fifty years, and it was difficult to imagine them living anywhere else.

"Goodbye, house," I whispered as I took a final look around. I knew this was the last time I would see my childhood home. A mixed bag of memories, good and bad, flew through my mind as I bade farewell to the place that had been home for my parents for so long. I hugged them goodbye with promises to call when my plane landed.

After returning to the Bay Area, I drove the twenty miles to San Ramon for my job interview. My legs were jumpy. Except for some phone interviews for my freelance writing and consulting jobs, I had not interviewed for a job for seven years, and I was feeling a little out of practice. I'd already completed the consulting company's online tests and editing exercises. The next step was meeting with the recruiter and the California director for the Seattle-based company. They had a big client in San Ramon that employed many of their consultants.

When I arrived for my interview, the recruiter greeted me.

"Unfortunately, Brad, our California director, will not be able to join us today. But he may want to set something up with you later."

"Sure, no problem." I hid my disappointment, wondering if it was a bad sign. Fortunately, the interview with the recruiter went well. It was a long-term contract job developing training courses and was expected to last six months to a year. It sounded like a good opportunity, and I was enthusiastic. After the interview, I received a phone call from the recruiter.

"Brad would like to have a phone interview with you. Can we schedule something?"

"Yes, that would be great!" I couldn't hide my enthusiasm. Apparently, the interview with Brad went well, because that led to a phone interview with the founder of the company. Shortly after that, I received a phone call from the recruiter. I was hired! My start date was August first, and the money was a lot more than I was making with my part-time aerial photo sales. Not only that, but they offered health insurance and a 401(k) plan, benefits I didn't have while traveling. I could save for retirement again, something I had not been doing while I was traveling because I wasn't making much money. Best of all, this job was much more interesting and challenging than the one I'd had before I started my travels, and writing was part of the job—a dream come true.

My motorhome traveling days were over. I would be staying put in the Bay Area for as long as this project lasted. I was ready to hang up the motorhome keys for a while and go back to a conventional lifestyle. I wanted to prepare for my financial future so I could travel where I wanted without worrying about money, and also have some continuity with relationships. Feeding my spirit with travel, adventure, and freedom had been very healing for me, and I was ready for the next phase of my life.

I called Jake, my manager with the aerial photo company.

"Sorry, Jake, but I received an offer I can't refuse. I won't be able to work for you anymore." I told him about my job.

"It sounds like an offer you have to take," Jake said. "I'm happy for you, and you are always welcome to come back and work for us again."

Although I felt a stitch of sadness at the closing of this chapter in my life, I was ready for a change. Oddly, this new opportunity was bringing me back to the Bay Area, where I'd started. To someone else, it might seem like I was going backward.

But things were different now—I was different. I was not the same person I had been when I started my traveling adventure.

Back in 2006, I'd set out for what I thought would be one year of travel in my motorhome. That one year turned into five years, and I was amazed that I had been able to continue my journey for that long. Traveling alone for five years in a motorhome was a life-changing experience for me. It was a time of tremendous personal growth. I discovered how easy it was to make friends with travelers and made new friendships that I treasured. I made mistakes—some heartbreaking—but I gained confidence and got to know myself better. I learned how to battle with the Green Monster and survive on the road by myself. I realized I could fit in wherever I wanted, and that we really don't need all of the stuff we fill our homes with in order to enjoy life. Most importantly, I learned that wonderful things can happen when you face your fears and take a leap. I was so grateful that I had not let fear prevent me from setting out on my solo journey or going to Baja for two months with people I barely knew.

I thought about the carefree child I had been in my early days, before I was old enough to pick up on the difficulties in our family. Somehow, that child had been buried beneath the papier-mâché layers of life struggles and disappointments that followed. It had taken this midlife journey to slowly peel away the gummed-up layers and get back to my authentic self. The person who could wonder at fireflies and delight in bioluminescence and whales. I could play, fall down, pick myself up, and go rolling down the path of life again, a happy person. I might get depressed again, but my experiences had taught me that I was stronger and more resilient and resourceful than I thought. If that storm came around again, I could weather it better next time.

I'd also found a new appreciation for nature, animals, and all of the wonderful places that this world has to offer.

HEIDI ELIASON

I'd regained hope, optimism, and a passion for life that I had
lost sight of for a while. I knew that even when life is dark and
gloomy, good things can be waiting just around the corner. I'd
found a lot of clarity about what was important to me and what
I wanted for the rest of my life. I knew that travel would always
be a big part of my life, but I was ready for a home base again.

A couple of weeks after starting my new job, Rylie woke
me up at two a.m. with a bark. He didn't usually bark during
the night, so I struggled to escape from the cobwebs of sleep.

"What's the matter, Rylie?" My voice was heavy with sleep.
I heard a loud crackling noise, then a thud on the roof of the
motorhome, and it rocked back and forth like a bucking
bronco. I didn't know what had happened. *Was that an
earthquake? But what was the crackling noise? Did power lines fall
on the motorhome?* Pins and needles shot through my veins as I
imagined a number of possible disasters. I got out of bed and
went to the door of the motorhome. I couldn't see anything
through the window in the door, so I turned on the outside
porch light. I saw a mass of pine branches right in front of the
door. That's when I realized the crackling noise was the sound
of splitting wood from the pine tree right next to my
motorhome.

I looked at Rylie. "You were trying to warn me, weren't
you, buddy? You're a good boy." I patted him on the head,
then got dressed and grabbed my flashlight. I couldn't get out
the motorhome door because the branches were blocking it, so
I went out the driver's-side door in the cab. I aimed the
flashlight toward the door of the motorhome and saw the entire
side of the motorhome was covered in tree branches. The
flashlight traveled up, and I saw two large branches suspended
over the roof of the motorhome. Part of the very large pine tree
had split off. I realized that Rylie and I were very lucky. If the
pine branches' hitting the ground had not stopped the fall of
the tree limbs, they would have crashed onto the motorhome

right above the bed where we slept. We could have been crushed if they came through the roof, or at least severely injured.

I told Rylie, "It's time to find another place to live. And we're staying in a hotel tonight." I packed up a few of our belongings, got Rylie in the car, and checked into a nearby hotel. The next morning, I returned to the motorhome to find the manager standing nearby.

"I have a crew on the way to cut those branches down," she said. "What happened?" I told her what I heard during the night and that I didn't feel comfortable staying in the motorhome with the tree limbs hanging over my bed, so we had gone to a hotel.

Once the branches and wood were removed, I could see the damage to the motorhome was surprisingly minimal, considering the size of the tree limbs. Just scratches, a few dents, and a puncture in the refrigerator vent. *I am so lucky.* Even though the damage was minor and we were fine, this just reinforced my desire for a sturdier home.

A couple of months later, we moved into a two-bedroom town house with a small, fenced yard. It was in a pretty area with mature trees, grass, and even a nearby pond with ducks and turtles where Rylie and I could walk every day. There was just one catch: there was no RV parking allowed at my new place.

I found a storage facility not far away that accepted RVs and got the Green Monster parked. Then I loaded the last of the things I needed from the motorhome into the car and started the engine. I glanced in the rearview mirror as I drove away, the familiar green stripes fading from view. As frustrated as I was with all of the malfunctioning components and expensive repairs, I had become very attached to the Green Monster during our five-year journey. It was my magic carpet. I had a lump in my throat as I drove away.

I pulled into the garage of my new home and opened the trunk. I made several trips inside the town house with the boxes that I'd carried around in the trunk for months. I set the boxes on the kitchen counter and carefully removed the dishes I'd bought in Visalia. I wasn't sure what they represented to me, but I felt happy just looking at them. I washed and dried the dishes, relieved to see they had not been damaged during those months riding around in the car. Then I stacked them neatly on the cupboard shelves and smiled as I closed the door.

EPILOGUE

BIRTHDAY GIFTS

JANUARY 2013

Life is constantly supporting us and giving us gifts. It's a matter of opening ourselves to that.

—Dan Millman

I t was January tenth, my birthday. My instructional design contract job had been extended, and the consulting company had just hired me as a full-time employee, after I'd worked for a year and a half as a contract employee. The work was interesting and challenging, and I was making a good salary. I had a fun social life with a nice circle of friends, some of whom I'd met through a hiking group. We hiked regularly, had parties, played games, and went dancing. Although I rarely traveled in the motorhome, I was starting to do more international trips, which satisfied my wanderlust.

Four months earlier, I'd gone to Peru with a new friend from the hiking group for a high-altitude trek to Machu Picchu in the Andes mountains. We hiked every day, stayed in quaint lodges at night, and even crossed a fifteen-thousand-foot mountain pass. High-altitude hiking was tough, but the payoff was huge. Machu Picchu had been number one on my bucket list for a long time, but I crossed it off as though it were

Mt. Everest. Life was good to me. The only thing missing was a partner to share my experiences with, something I had wanted for a long time. But I wasn't lonely. I had lots of fun friends to keep me company, plus I got to see Cammie regularly again. I was happy, and that was quite a transformation from the woman I had been eight years earlier, when I was envying the homeless people.

The morning of my birthday, I opened my email to see the Canadian's name. My pulse still quickened when I saw it. Maybe some inner part of me recognized the danger this man presented. He wanted to wish me a happy birthday, but it was also a letter of apology. He told me how sorry he was for the way he'd behaved. After being married for so long and finally getting a divorce, he told me he had been like a kid in a candy store. I could understand, but it didn't change anything. I didn't want to be with someone who lied to me. I wanted someone I could trust. I thanked him for the birthday wishes but told him we were both better off now, so it was all good. I wished him a happy life. As I sent the email, I smiled, knowing it was true. I *was* happier now.

My best friend had asked weeks ago what I wanted to do to celebrate this birthday. "I want to get some friends together to go to dinner and dancing," I told her. My friend's former neighbor was the lead singer in a band that was playing at a restaurant and bar a half hour away. I'd heard the band play a few times, and they were good. After dinner, we all packed the dance floor until the band was done playing. My friend had brought a big birthday cake, so we invited the band members to have some cake. Although I had met the lead singer on numerous occasions, I had never met the rest of the band. As we were chatting and eating cake before leaving, I introduced myself to the tall guy standing next to me, the bass player.

"Hi, I'm Dan," he said, shaking my hand. "Happy birthday."

"Thanks. You guys are really good." We chatted for a few minutes. "When do you play again?" I asked.

"We're playing in two weeks at Dallimonti's in Pleasant Hill. You should come."

"I live in Pleasant Hill, so maybe I will."

"Good. Maybe I'll see you in a couple of weeks, then." He smiled and squeezed my hand.

He seemed solid and genuine, like someone I could count on. I had a spring in my step as I walked out the door.

Made in the USA
Coppell, TX
27 February 2023

13468931R00163